Oaks

of

Righteousness

A Practical 31-Day Journey for the Radical God Chaser

Volume I

Malachi C. Steele

Published by:

Connect with the author @ malachicsteele@gmail.com

ISBN: 978-1-958404-31-7 (paperback)

Table of Contents

Introduction

The daily altar of devotion and meditation to the Lord has been decimated over the years by the increased demands of life. We spend more time commuting to work, longer hours in the office to appease the expectations placed on us, more time watching television or otherwise occupied by social media and the different apps from our mobile and semi-mobile devices. It has become a world filled with busyness and distractions to the detriment of our spiritual growth.

We must rebuild these altars in our homes and retrain ourselves to include devotion and mediation—and I would like to add communion—in our daily lives. Life is more than our jobs and the many distractions that consume our lives.

This Practical 31-Day Journey for the Radical God Chaser series was designed to aid in our attempt to re-establish the altars in our homes and daily lives as we make it mandatory, among all other demands, to pursue the heart and mind of God, regardless of how busy and distracted our lives have become.

As I share different levels of my own journey with you, you will get an opportunity to engage with God in prayer, meditate on the thoughts I share, and partake of the holy communion. Don't be limited by the short prayers I share in this book. Keep on praying as the Spirit leads you during your time of devotion. Make sure you take the time to be silent and listen as well. Allow the voice of God to saturate your being in those powerful moments of stillness. I believe this will radically change your life.

Are you ready?

Day 1
Oaks Of Righteousness

Interestingly, the Bible refers to trees a lot. There are trees in the beginning (Genesis), and there is a tree in the end (Revelation), whose leaves are for the healing of the nations (see Revelation 22:2). There are even references to men as trees in Scripture.

They spread before me like palm groves, like gardens by the riverside. They are like tall trees planted by the Lord, like cedars beside the waters. (Numbers 24:6 – NLT).

There is a story told of a blind man who met Jesus. When Jesus first touched him, he saw men walking like trees. We assume his sight was not fully restored but never gave consideration that his eyes were open to see from or into another dimension.

My favourite Scripture: **To all who mourn in Israel, he will give a crown of beauty for ashes, a joyous blessing instead of mourning, festive praise instead of despair. In their righteousness, they will be like great oaks that the Lord has planted for his own glory. (Isaiah 61:3 – NLT).**

What if we are trees planted on the earth, in a spiritual sense of course?

They are like trees planted along the riverbank, bearing fruit each season. Their leaves never wither, and they prosper in all they do. (Psalm 1:3 – NLT).

How deep are your roots? From where do you draw sustenance? What is your source? Are we attractive to the world? Can they feed on our fruits and leave being restored and healed? Can those we encounter experience the life that flows through us?

We are planted where we are for a reason. Oaks of Righteousness are scattered all over the world. Our greatest ministry is not within the four walls of the church; it is literally everywhere else, in every place where we are planted.

We may not be comfortable where we are; we may want to escape at the first opportunity that presents itself; we may pray for Friday to come quickly where we are planted; we may want to be transferred to another location, but God planted you there for a reason.

People feed on us every day. Our lives bring healing by virtue of who we are in God, and we don't even know it. Some people who touch us or cross our paths should have died, but the life that flowed from us and into them changed that, and we don't even know it.

Life flows from you every day into the world around you. If your greatest ambition and goal is about you: what you get from life, what you achieve in life, how much possessions you acquire in life, then you are not thinking big enough; you are not thinking God-thoughts. There is no tree that eats its own fruit.

Prayer and Communion

Lord, help me to accept that You have planted me where I am so I can bear fruit for the nurturing of others. As I approach the Lord's table, may You solidify this truth in my heart and mind. Amen.

(Continue praying as the Spirit leads. You can pray in tongues, if you know how. Then take some time to just sit quietly, eyes close, and listen. Silence your mind for a little while and approach the darkness you see without thought, and just listen. You may hear something, or you may not. When you are ready, open your eyes and take communion).

Lord, You said, as I eat and drink the flesh and blood of the Son of Man, I have life in me. Your flesh is real food and your blood is real drink. By eating your flesh and drinking your blood I enter into You and You into me. In the same way that the Father sent You here and You live because of Him, so when I make a meal of You, I will live because of You. You are the Bread from heaven. When I eat this Bread, I will live always.[1]

Lord, this is Your instruction to me. On the night of Your betrayal, you took bread. Having given thanks, You broke it and said, "This is my body, broken for you. Do this to remember me." After supper, You did the same thing with the cup: "This cup is my blood, my new covenant with you. Each time you drink this cup, remember me."

I declare that every time I eat this bread and drink this cup, I reenact in words and actions Your death, Lord. I will be drawn back to this meal again and again until You return. By faith, I eat Your body and drink Your blood.[2]

---

[1] see John 6:53-58 - MSG
[2] see 1 Corinthians 11:24-28 - MSG

Day 2
My Journey Beyond

I have been asked certain questions repeatedly, so I thought I would answer these questions here. I want to sum up my beliefs with a few scriptures, and a very basic abridged version of my journey over the last maybe ten years:

By this is love perfected with us, so that we may have confidence for the day of judgment, because as he is so also are we in this world. (1 John 4:17 – ESV).

The "He" referenced here is talking about Jesus. This sentence alone destroyed much of my initial doctrinal beliefs. Most of our doctrine is based on a separationist perception that goes against scripture. By virtue of what Jesus did, He has made us one with Him as He is one with the Godhead. We may have been vile and insignificant wretches before Christ, but when we said "Yes" to Jesus, all that changed. His identity and nature became ours, enabling us to do the same things He did. Yet, doing what Jesus did is only the foundation of our journey as Christians (See Hebrews 5:12-14, 6:1-6).

Please note that "enlightenment" is considered a new age word, similar to mysticism.

I want to quote a scripture that I believe with all my heart is the standard of the church:

Later He appeared to the eleven as they sat at the table; and He rebuked their unbelief and hardness of heart, because they did not believe those who had seen Him after He had risen. And He said to them, "Go into all the world and preach the gospel to every creature. He who believes and is baptized will be saved; but he who does not believe will be condemned. And these signs will follow those who believe: In My name they will cast out demons; they will speak with new tongues; they will take up serpents; and if they drink anything deadly, it will by no means hurt them; they will lay hands on the sick, and they will recover." So then, after the Lord had spoken to them, He was received up into heaven, and sat down at the right hand of God. And they went out and preached everywhere, the Lord working with them and confirming the word through the accompanying signs. Amen. (Mark 16:14-20 – NKJV).

The subtitle of this passage is the "Great Commission," yet when we as a church refer to the great commission, we use the scripture in Matthew:

Go therefore and make disciples of all the nations, baptizing them in the name of the Father and of the Son and of the Holy Spirit. (Matthew 28:19 – NKJV).

But this is just a part of the mandate of the church. What happened to the rest in Mark? This was how the early church operated, so when did we cease operating like that?

So, I can hear your concerns, and they are very valid. The mindset my language challenges has given rise to a lot of difficulties in my personal life. The use of the word "mysticism," for example. I do prefer to say Christian Spirituality instead of Christian Mysticism because of the negative connotations assigned to the word.

Yes, there is a counterfeit, secular, worldly version of mysticism, but it means if there is a counterfeit version, it most certainly must have been derived from the original authentic version. This is true straight across the board for other new age words/practices like meditation, enlightenment, out-of-body experiences, etc. The authentic version of all these practices we have surrendered to the "other side" is replete throughout Scripture: New and Old Testament.

As a matter of fact, the early church had a lot of "mystical" experiences:

It is doubtless not profitable for me to boast. I will come to visions and revelations of the Lord: I know a man in Christ who fourteen years ago—whether in the body I do not know, or whether out of the body I do not know, God knows—such a one was caught up to the third heaven. And I know such a man—whether in the body or out of the body I do not know, God knows— how he was caught up into Paradise and heard inexpressible words, which it is not lawful for a man to utter. (2 Corinthians 12:1-4 – NKJV).

If I point to mysticism, it is in no way pointing to the fake version with the use of tarot cards, stones, and whatever. But we should never have surrendered what is rightfully ours because some corrupt people corrupted what it truly meant to be mystical. My use of the word speaks of our union with God (not my idea, of course. Not even my words).

I do not pray for these alone, but also for those who will believe in Me through their word; that they all may be one, as You, Father, are in Me, and I in You; that they also may be one in Us, that the world may believe that You sent Me. And the glory which You gave Me I have given them, that they may be one

just as We are one: I in them, and You in Me; that they may be made perfect in one, and that the world may know that You have sent Me, and have loved them as You have loved Me. (John 17:20-23 – NKJV).

So, my greatest challenge now is, if the church as we know it now could change this world, then the world would have been changing and not getting worse. I believe in the glorious, radiant church that is spoken about in Ephesians that Jesus will present to the Father, and I do not believe we accomplish this through physical death. I also believe the church is far from this reality because we have made church about programs, activities, positions, and not a community of people seeking after the heart and mind of God. In other words, whether God shows up or not, we are having church.

I explore these difficult topics because I believe the church as we know it has deviated from the original model Jesus established, and we have so many doctrines to back it up, but none of it is really Biblical. We cannot say the apostolic and prophetic died with the apostles because the Bible never said that. We cannot say the age of miracles, signs, and wonders died with the apostles because the Bible never said that. I also know that human beings can do these things outside of a relationship with Jesus, so I fully believe in walking in the fullness of what Jesus has accomplished, and all

17

these wonderful things, a true mystical/spiritual life, with signs following, and our capacity to manifest God in this realm must also flow out of our relationship with the Godhead.

I believe many believers live under a false identity that is based on our fallenness and not on what Christ accomplished. Our identity is in Him; it actually belongs to Him, but He has gifted us with it, for example, holiness, perfection, righteousness, and forgiveness. This is why I use affirmations.

If God is love, for example, and I am filled with God (which is what we teach is the baptism of the Holy Spirit), then what do I become? Isn't the vessel defined by what is inside it?

The church is not the building but the people. We are all members of the body of Christ, and each a temple of God. I believe the church needs reformation and not a revival. What is the difference? Revival is like a fire that quickly blazes up but eventually dissipates. We have seen a lot of this in the history of the church. Reformation speaks to changes that will last.

There is a spiritual reformation coming to the church, and it will cause a division. As it was in Jesus' day, so shall it be in our day. Jesus is building His church, and every believer will have a choice to make: Will we choose to walk with Jesus or remain in the man-made, man-inspired, man-maintained version of the church?

Prayer and Communion

Lord, help me to understand that I don't just have access to this world, but I have access to the world beyond time. May I draw from that world as You did when You walked this earth. Amen.

(Continue praying as the Spirit leads. You can pray in tongues, if you know how. Then take some time to just sit quietly, eyes close, and listen. Silence your mind for a little while and approach the darkness you see without thought, and just listen. You may hear something, or you may not. When you are ready, open your eyes and take communion).

Lord, You said, as I eat and drink the flesh and blood of the Son of Man, I have life in me. Your flesh is real food and your blood is real drink. By eating your flesh and drinking your blood I enter into You and You into me. In the same way that the Father sent You here and You live because of Him, so when I make a meal of You, I will live because of You. You are the Bread from heaven. When I eat this Bread, I will live always.[3]

---

[3] see John 6:53-58 - MSG

Lord, this is Your instruction to me. On the night of Your betrayal, you took bread. Having given thanks, You broke it and said, "This is my body, broken for you. Do this to remember me." After supper, You did the same thing with the cup: "This cup is my blood, my new covenant with you. Each time you drink this cup, remember me."

I declare that every time I eat this bread and drink this cup, I reenact in words and actions Your death, Lord. I will be drawn back to this meal again and again until You return. By faith, I eat Your body and drink Your blood.[4]

---

[4] see 1 Corinthians 11:24-28 - MSG

Day 3
Prophetic Insight: A Dying Church

I was listening to a mystic father teach, and he said the church as we know it must die for Jesus to build His church. He alludes to the reality that the structure and function of the present-day church is man-established and man-led, not Spirit-led. Anyone who disagrees with this must explain why there are so many denominations if this is not true.

So, I want to have a candid conversation, if you have the time and tenacity to indulge me in such. I grew up in the church...Pentecostal, Tongue Speaking, Holy-Rollers (holiness in relation to dress codes, no jewelry, etc). I have seen and experienced and observed. The first thing to note is our capacity to look past the obvious to embrace an acceptable modus operandi. Even when it is screaming, "this is not working," we still do it, and even worse, we expect different results, eventually, every time. Twenty years later, same story, same results, still no change. No one is radical enough to pull the church in the direction it needs to go because they don't want the responsibility of nurturing a new "baby." It is much easier to believe and accept what everyone else believes and accepts than it is to steward a new move of God.

Alright. Fine. Personally, I want the truth, so let me go ahead and pursue that. Ooops! The result: hostility, indifference, cold shoulders, criticisms, gossip, backbiting, and isolation. What this says is that to think differently is to accept exile. So we have this inherited doctrine that lacks power and authenticity that we embrace as the ultimate truth, yet it causes us to experience far less than what the early church experienced, but somehow we convince ourselves that what we believe is correct though we have no real basis for it. The reality is, someone told us what to believe. How do I know this: Because to believe differently is to come under fire by someone who thinks it is their duty to enforce a belief system they inherited but have never really proven. God did say we should test everything before deciding how authentic it is. I tested "sound doctrine" when I was addicted to a particular sin, when I felt I was oppressed by demons, when I was sick, when I was going through depression, when I had lost all hope, when I was confused about life; it did nothing but keep me in church, which is a good thing, but I was in need of more. Essentially, what we are saying is, doctrine has not changed, but there are just some things God no longer does. I would be fine with this, if it were true, but it is not true because the Bible does not support that thinking. What if it is the flip side that is true, that God is the same and still wants to do the same, but our doctrine is off? Are we brave enough to explore this possibility?

I am going to assume that the answer is no, so let's proceed. Is the church dying? Let's examine this. In ten years, we have seen fewer people come to the Lord. Most of those who do have found themselves in church because there is a need that they wanted to address. So their decision is seemingly a temporal one because most don't stay in church. We count them as the sheep that came to the fold, we celebrate, we add them to the number, but ignore the fact that they have left.

The message is "Get saved or go to hell." That is the elevator pitch for making converts. It is not the love of God because while we can point to the ultimate sacrifice over 2000 years ago, there is nothing in the present that we can show to demonstrate God's love now. The sick are still sick; the dead are still dead; the lame is still lame; the blind still blind; the ones suffering hopelessness, anguish, trauma, and anxiety can barely find any relief. But we tell them to get saved or go to hell. We may tell them to come to Jesus, and He will fix it, but there is no contingency if the problem is not fixed, so they leave believing Christianity to be a hoax. Can you blame them? They are getting more tangible results from the occult world. Why should they believe in a God who seems less powerful than those who are operating independently of God? Even worse, our concept of hell being a place where an angry God will burn and torment His prodigal sons and daughters for all eternity seems to contradict God's nature, so how about we revisit that stuff? Uhm? Hm? I am sure there is a hell but is it what we think?

Is the church dying? Young people predominantly show little to no interest in church. Most of them are there because a senior family member is there. Those who are there, wonder why they are there, and if this is what we want them to believe is "purpose." They sit in the congregation, observing, fantasizing about what is beyond the walls. They feel caged, restricted, shackled; they want adventure; they want to explore; they want truth. We tell them, ignore your desires, forget your dreams, pay no attention to your thoughts, ask no question, ignore your passions; just sit, survive, get old and die or be raptured, whichever comes first. The older folks, who are already halfway or more out of here, want the young people to be like them, sing the same songs, read the same scriptures, believe the same doctrine… Let me get off this point so I don't offend.

There is a culture that is in Scripture that is missing from the church. This is the worst part of this scenario for me. The Book of Acts ends with the supernatural; Paul was all about the demonstration of the power of the Holy Spirit; and John closed the canon with an out-of-body experience and a high level prophetic, accurate discourse. The five-fold (Apostle, Evangelist, Pastor, Teacher and Prophet) was very much a foundational principle of the early church to the very last letter of the Bible. Yet, somehow, in the last 2000 years, the church decided that a lot of that stuff was no longer relevant. Now these are gifts that Jesus Himself gives, one; and two, Jesus Himself said He would build the church; so why did we take matters into our own hands and create a version of Christianity that we have seemingly been okay with for centuries, even though it is starkly different from Biblical text? It means we have embraced a non-Biblical culture, and we have the doctrine to support it. Where did we get that doctrine from, if it is not supported Biblically? Why did we settle for anything less than what was introduced to us in Scripture? Why do we continue to settle when there are so many voices on the earth now groaning and crying for authentic Christianity?

Here is the prophetic insight. The principle of death and resurrection must be applied to the church in a similar way that the physical body must die for there to be a resurrection. If our bodies are not what it is supposed to be now and there are two ways for it to change; either supernaturally, in the twinkling of an eye, or through death and resurrection, then the same thing must apply to the body of Christ. We can fight this tongue, tooth, and nail, but the death of the church is inevitable, but it is not the end. It will be the end of a lot of things, but it will be a beautiful beginning for the unfolding and manifesting of the true, radiant church. The truth still remains: Jesus will build His church and the gates of hell will not prevail against it.

Prayer and Communion

Lord, You have called me to be a member of Your church. Open my eyes to see the truth and not be blindsided by even those with good intentions. Help me to see myself as a member of the body of Christ and to know the role I must play for the overall benefit of the body. Amen.

(Continue praying as the Spirit leads. You can pray in tongues, if you know how. Then take some time to just sit quietly, eyes close, and listen. Silence your mind for a little while and approach the darkness you see without thought, and just listen. You may hear something, or you may not. When you are ready, open your eyes and take communion).

Lord, You said, as I eat and drink the flesh and blood of the Son of Man, I have life in me. Your flesh is real food and your blood is real drink. By eating your flesh and drinking your blood I enter into You and You into me. In the same way that the Father sent You here and You live because of Him, so when I make a meal of

You, I will live because of You. You are the Bread from heaven. When I eat this Bread, I will live always.[5]

Lord, this is Your instruction to me. On the night of Your betrayal, you took bread. Having given thanks, You broke it and said, "This is my body, broken for you. Do this to remember me." After supper, You did the same thing with the cup: "This cup is my blood, my new covenant with you. Each time you drink this cup, remember me."

I declare that every time I eat this bread and drink this cup, I reenact in words and actions Your death, Lord. I will be drawn back to this meal again and again until You return. By faith, I eat Your body and drink Your blood.[6]

---

[5] see John 6:53-58 - MSG
[6] see 1 Corinthians 11:24-28 - MSG

Day 4
The Poor, Wise Man

Now there was found in it a poor wise man, and he by his wisdom delivered the city. Yet no one remembered that same poor man. (Ecclesiastes 9:15 – NKJV).

I was meditating on this Scripture one day, when God began speaking to me. I usually use this scripture to justify my desire not to be poor. I saw poverty as a curse (and to some extent, it is), but how I viewed this scripture is that if we wish to have great influence and be remembered, we cannot do it from the perspective of poverty. A poor man is not remembered, regardless of what he did.

So, in my mind, I needed to drive a certain kind of car and live somewhat of a lavish lifestyle to be seen by men and considered a voice of influence in the world of men. I was even told that based on this scripture, I should not expect anyone to really listen to me speak on faith because it is not reflected in the kind of car that I drove, how I dressed, and my reality of being indebted.

So, I was complaining within myself, thinking my outward accumulated possessions needed to reflect a faith that produced material things in order to be seen, heard, and remembered, when the Lord spoke gently to my soul. He said I was missing the point. "How so, Lord?"

"The poor, wise man saved the city, and he was okay with not being known, seen, or remembered."

Heaven's perspective of us and what we do is very different from the earthly, human perspective. Where we see poverty, God sees an abundance of wealth and influence. The man was poor, and he was wise, and the entire city benefitted from his wisdom. He may not have received a pat on the back, accolades, the best seats in the house, or an abundance of praise from the lips of men, but his story was impactful enough to be recorded in the records of human history. His name may not be on the lips or the pen of men, but he is known by God.

Your social status has nothing to do with what God has called you to do. You don't need to be seen or rewarded by men. Your accolades and recognition come from the One who created you. Do not feel pressured to accumulate possessions or spend foolishly on maintaining a certain social status to increase your influence. It is nothing but a smoke screen. Humble yourself enough to change a nation or the world and not be remembered.

Prayer and Communion

Lord, help me to be okay with just being seen and appreciated by You. I know what You see is not the same thing others see. You see me in a light that I may not even see myself, but what You see is all that matters. Help me to see me through Your eyes, and appreciate me for who I am. May I find my identity, calling, and purpose in You only. Amen.

(Continue praying as the Spirit leads. You can pray in tongues, if you know how. Then take some time to just sit quietly, eyes close, and listen. Silence your mind for a little while and approach the darkness you see without thought, and just listen. You may hear something, or you may not. When you are ready, open your eyes and take communion).

Lord, You said, as I eat and drink the flesh and blood of the Son of Man, I have life in me. Your flesh is real food and your blood is real drink. By eating your flesh and drinking your blood I enter into You and You into me. In the same way that the Father sent You here and You live because of Him, so when I make a meal of

You, I will live because of You. You are the Bread from heaven. When I eat this Bread, I will live always. [7]

Lord, this is Your instruction to me. On the night of Your betrayal, you took bread. Having given thanks, You broke it and said, "This is my body, broken for you. Do this to remember me." After supper, You did the same thing with the cup: "This cup is my blood, my new covenant with you. Each time you drink this cup, remember me."

I declare that every time I eat this bread and drink this cup, I reenact in words and actions Your death, Lord. I will be drawn back to this meal again and again until You return. By faith, I eat Your body and drink Your blood. [8]

---

[7] see John 6:53-58 - MSG
[8] see 1 Corinthians 11:24-28 - MSG

Day 5
We Are God's Gift to Creation And To Himself

Remove people from this world, and what do you have left? Nothing. The plant life would die. The animals would die, and there would be nothing left but a wasteland devoid of life. So, technically, the world does revolve around you.

If there were no humans, God would still be God, but creation would cease to exist if you were not here. God will never give up on you because you are that important to Him.

For the earnest expectation of the creation eagerly waits for the revealing of the sons of God. For the creation was subjected to futility, not willingly, but because of Him who subjected it in hope; because the creation itself also will be delivered from the bondage of corruption into the glorious liberty of the children of God. For we know that the whole creation groans and labors with birth pangs together until now. (Romans 8:19-22 – NKJV).

When man fell, creation fell. God subjected creation to man so creation does not rule over man. Creation can never return to its full capacity and functionality without the emergence of the matured sons of God. Neither can God operate in His fullest capacity and functionality without the emergence of the matured sons of God.

If it was God's job to fix creation, then creation would have been fixed and the world would have been better. But it is not His job, so God is waiting on the same thing creation is waiting on. But God has not left us as orphans.

We are chosen, royal, holy, and special, and because we are God's gift, He assumes the responsibility to take us through the process to maturity. The giver of the gift is always the one who determines the condition and value of the gift.

Prayer and Communion

Lord, help me to not lose sight of my true value. I am a special gift that You have given to Yourself and to creation. Help me manifest that which You have deposited in me. Freely I have received, and freely I give. Amen.

(Continue praying as the Spirit leads. You can pray in tongues, if you know how. Then take some time to just sit quietly, eyes close, and listen. Silence your mind for a little while and approach the darkness you see without thought, and just listen. You may hear something, or you may not. When you are ready, open your eyes and take communion).

Lord, You said, as I eat and drink the flesh and blood of the Son of Man, I have life in me. Your flesh is real food and your blood is real drink. By eating your flesh and drinking your blood I enter into You and You into me. In the same way that the Father sent You here and You live because of Him, so when I make a meal of You, I will live because of You. You are the Bread from heaven. When I eat this Bread, I will live always.[9]

Lord, this is Your instruction to me. On the night of Your betrayal, you took bread. Having given thanks, You broke it and said, "This is my body, broken for you. Do this to remember me." After supper, You did the same thing with the cup: "This cup is my blood, my new covenant with you. Each time you drink this cup, remember me."

I declare that every time I eat this bread and drink this cup, I reenact in words and actions Your death, Lord. I

---

[9] see John 6:53-58 - MSG

will be drawn back to this meal again and again until You return. By faith, I eat Your body and drink Your blood.[10]

---

[10] see 1 Corinthians 11:24-28 - MSG

Day 6
You Were Created to be Great

You are of God, little children, and have overcome them, because He who is in you is greater than he who is in the world. (1 John 4:4 – NKJV).

I know how we interpret this scripture in 1 John 4:4, but I want to put a different spin on it. Your soul is greater than your body, because it is from your soul that the life of God flows, and I believe when something goes wrong with the soul, that is how the body shuts down and dies.

The soul is directly connected to God and contains all that God is, though in seed form. The soul is perfect, righteous, holy, and extremely powerful, and is also immortal.

The desires of the body can hinder the flow of the soul. When we harbour emotional wounds, such as unforgiveness, offence, lust, pride, etc, it becomes something negative in the body. There are people who believe strongly that unforgiveness is tied to cancer, though there is no explanation then, if this is true, why innocent children are born with cancer. It does make sense though that in a body, where a holy, god-like soul lives, unrighteousness will produce a negative effect, not on the soul, but in the body.

So, God's commands not to indulge in certain things is not to deny us pleasure, but to stop us from hindering our greatness because you were created to be great.

In my studies, I have concluded that we may be living in the age of the ungodly, because Gentiles have a natural propensity towards ungodliness and atheism, and the ungodly are ruling the world, but there is coming a shift, and the age of the righteous will begin, and we are being prepared for that.

You were created to be great, and you need to overcome the fear and reservations that come with accepting this reality. You have so much to offer.

Prayer and Communion

Lord, You said greater is He who is in me than he who is in the world. I feel so small sometimes, especially when faced with giants, but may I be reminded of how wonderful and awesome You have created me to be. Made in Your image and likeness, I embody Your divine nature, and am empowered to manifest Your greatness in this world. Activate the gifts you have placed in me so I can function at my fullest capacity. Amen.

(Continue praying as the Spirit leads. You can pray in tongues, if you know how. Then take some time to just sit quietly, eyes close, and listen. Silence your mind for a little while and approach the darkness you see without thought, and just listen. You may hear something, or you may not. When you are ready, open your eyes and take communion).

Lord, You said, as I eat and drink the flesh and blood of the Son of Man, I have life in me. Your flesh is real food and your blood is real drink. By eating your flesh and drinking your blood I enter into You and You into me. In the same way that the Father sent You here and You live because of Him, so when I make a meal of You, I will live because of You. You are the Bread from heaven. When I eat this Bread, I will live always.[11]

Lord, this is Your instruction to me. On the night of Your betrayal, you took bread. Having given thanks, You broke it and said, "This is my body, broken for you. Do this to remember me." After supper, You did the same thing with the cup: "This cup is my blood, my new covenant with you. Each time you drink this cup, remember me."

---

[11] see John 6:53-58 - MSG

I declare that every time I eat this bread and drink this cup, I reenact in words and actions Your death, Lord. I will be drawn back to this meal again and again until You return. By faith, I eat Your body and drink Your blood.[12]

Day 7
The Gospel is Supernatural

In meditation a few years ago, I had a profound experience. I went fishing with Jesus. He was jovial and fun to be around, but He was catching fish after fish, and I was not catching anything. He taught me a valuable lesson that day when I asked Him what He was doing differently. He said, "It's all about the bait. You cannot catch fish without having the right bait."

My mind went to Peter pulling that lame man to his feet at the gate beautiful. After which, he preached and 3,000 people got saved. The miracle was the bait.

Jesus says, I will make you fishers of men. That is interesting when you think about it. You cannot go fishing without having the correct bait. Because the supernatural is missing from our churches, we had to depend on the powers of persuasion, and the church's bait became, "Get saved or you are going to hell." Many of us got saved out of a fear of going to hell— which we still struggle with to this day—and not for our love of a God who is able to do above and beyond what we can ask, think or imagine.

40

So what happens to the church when our powers of persuasion no longer scares the population...few people get saved...fewer people remain long-term after getting saved. Unless we are able to do as Paul did, do as the disciples did, do as Jesus did, our ministering will not yield the kind of harvest we would want because the gospel is supernatural. You cannot separate the two.

So, here is my issue. I believe in the supernatural...we believe, we pursue it, we go after it, but we still see so little manifestations. Why is this? So, I look at one example in Scripture where Jesus had this challenge in one town.

When He had come to His own country, He taught them in their synagogue, so that they were astonished and said, "Where did this Man get this wisdom and these mighty works? Is this not the carpenter's son? Is not His mother called Mary? And His brothers James, Joses, Simon, and Judas? And His sisters, are they not all with us? Where then did this Man get all these things?" So they were offended at Him. But Jesus said to them, "A prophet is not without honor except in his own country and in his own house." Now He did not do many mighty works there because of their unbelief. (Matthew 13:54-58 – NKJV).

So, we struggle with this very serious issue of unbelief, where you can have all the faith in the world and zero doubt, but if you are operating in an environment of unbelief...very little manifestations. So, the greatest hindrance to the supernatural is unbelief...plain and simple. We can fix this in ourselves, but we also need to fix it in others because unbelief is an assassin to the supernatural. If this is true for Jesus, how much more us.

So I say to us, develop a supernatural mindset and a journey of faith in your home, with your family, with your neighbors, among your friends first...start there, perfect it there so it can be carried over into our churches.

Prayer and Communion

Lord, help me to accept that the same works You did, I can do. Even greater works, You said. May this become my living reality. Help me to manifest Your love, Your heart and mind so those I encounter will encounter You. Amen.

(Continue praying as the Spirit leads. You can pray in tongues, if you know how. Then take some time to just sit quietly, eyes close, and listen. Silence your mind for a little while and approach the darkness you see without thought, and just listen. You may hear

something, or you may not. When you are ready, open your eyes and take communion).

Lord, You said, as I eat and drink the flesh and blood of the Son of Man, I have life in me. Your flesh is real food and your blood is real drink. By eating your flesh and drinking your blood I enter into You and You into me. In the same way that the Father sent You here and You live because of Him, so when I make a meal of You, I will live because of You. You are the Bread from heaven. When I eat this Bread, I will live always. [13]

Lord, this is Your instruction to me. On the night of Your betrayal, you took bread. Having given thanks, You broke it and said, "This is my body, broken for you. Do this to remember me." After supper, You did the same thing with the cup: "This cup is my blood, my new covenant with you. Each time you drink this cup, remember me."

I declare that every time I eat this bread and drink this cup, I reenact in words and actions Your death, Lord. I will be drawn back to this meal again and again until You return. By faith, I eat Your body and drink Your blood. [14]

---

[13] see John 6:53-58 - MSG
[14] see 1 Corinthians 11:24-28 - MSG

Day 8
The Power of Communion

If you study the early church, you realize that they met in individual homes daily and broke bread. It occurred every time they met, and they were meeting daily; and so they were breaking bread daily. They may have met three, four times for the day, and each time they would break bread. So, it was almost as if they cojoined the idea of communion with eating. Maybe that is why we bless our food, so that it gets transmuted and becomes something else. In breaking of bread with somebody else in that moment, we can actually be thinking about what Jesus Christ did in His body for our redemption. It is a beautiful and powerful thing.

I assume I'm addressing believers now who are mature. Draw your own conclusions: When we drink the cup of blessing, aren't we taking into ourselves the blood, the very life, of Christ? And isn't it the same with the loaf of bread we break and eat? Don't we take into ourselves the body, the very life, of Christ? Because there is one loaf, our many-ness becomes one-ness—Christ doesn't become fragmented in us. Rather, we become unified in him.

We don't reduce Christ to what we are; he raises us to what he is. That's basically what happened even in old Israel—those who ate the sacrifices offered on God's altar entered into God's action at the altar. (1 Corinthians 10:15-18 – MSG).

Communion is the only thing that Jesus left on earth that literally combines heaven and earth into one. It represents the body of Christ, and it represents the blood of Christ. When we take communion, we partake in His nature, partake in Him as a person; we feast on Him, basically. Yes, it is hard to find the language to describe what goes on, but I think Paul does a good job. In taking His body into our body, we take the life of God into our body. We take the life of God inside our physical body. I believe that in doing this, this is how we become partakers of God's divine nature.

This is how our DNA becomes one with God's DNA. This is how our own blood becomes one with God's blood. This is how our life becomes one with God's life. This is how we begin to experience union with God. This is how we access the healing virtue in God. I believe most of the writers of the Bible understood the power of communion.

If physical food provides nourishment to the physical body, then communion is nourishment to the soul/spirit, and the suggestion here is that communion should be a daily practice for believers.

Prayer and Communion

Lord, help me to understand that in the same way the physical body cannot sustain itself without physical food, I need to feast on You to receive nourishment for my soul and spirit. I may do it alone or with others, but may I experience the full benefits of partaking in Your body and blood. Amen.

(Continue praying as the Spirit leads. You can pray in tongues, if you know how. Then take some time to just sit quietly, eyes close, and listen. Silence your mind for a little while and approach the darkness you see without thought, and just listen. You may hear something, or you may not. When you are ready, open your eyes and take communion).

Lord, You said, as I eat and drink the flesh and blood of the Son of Man, I have life in me. Your flesh is real food and your blood is real drink. By eating your flesh and drinking your blood I enter into You and You into me. In the same way that the Father sent You here and You live because of Him, so when I make a meal of

You, I will live because of You. You are the Bread from heaven. When I eat this Bread, I will live always.[15]

Lord, this is Your instruction to me. On the night of Your betrayal, you took bread. Having given thanks, You broke it and said, "This is my body, broken for you. Do this to remember me." After supper, You did the same thing with the cup: "This cup is my blood, my new covenant with you. Each time you drink this cup, remember me."

I declare that every time I eat this bread and drink this cup, I reenact in words and actions Your death, Lord. I will be drawn back to this meal again and again until You return. By faith, I eat Your body and drink Your blood.[16]

---

[15] see John 6:53-58 - MSG
[16] see 1 Corinthians 11:24-28 - MSG

Day 9
There Is More

I love people. I love them to the point that it tears my heart apart when I see them living way below their potential; even worse, they have little interest in what that potential is, the fullness of which is still a mystery. The Lord has been educating me, not about Him so much, but about what it means to be human. I have been pulled all the way back to 'original intent.' What was God thinking when He made man? What did we look like? How did we function?

Science confirms that we only use 10% of our brain capacity. It is also a proven fact that our minds are incredibly powerful and can determine how we live and our functionality. If you examine all that a man has done with only 10% brain capacity, how can we ever sit contented that what we know is all there is to know? I have developed sympathy for atheists who would cross their legs and confidently declare that there is no God. It takes a whole lot of faith to do that, and most of them are eloquent speakers whose words cut deep like a sword. You cannot out-argue them, but our existence, or God's existence for that matter, was never meant to be decided by a verbal debate.

The issue I am having is that there is so much more, but I am not convinced that we want more. The deeper I dig into the truth is the more I realize that the foundation of Christianity is mystical in nature. Yes, I said it. It is the only conclusion that finally makes sense to me. The Bible was written by people whom God either chose to pull out of the basic stuff, or people who were content to seek after the more. There was nothing ordinary about any of the writers of Scripture, though one would be forced to argue, what exactly should ordinary look like? Enoch, for example, transcended human traditions and cultures to the extreme that he walked with God so closely that he never saw death. Yet, it is appointed unto men once to die, but after that the judgment. But, we see a few people who have cheated death, for example, Elijah.

The last remaining Emissary wrote the last book of the Bible, and it is assumed that he died, even though Jesus had mentioned that just maybe he wouldn't. Do we ever think about these things? I am talking about the possibility of walking with God to the extreme that the natural laws no longer apply, to some extent. I am talking about having that face-to-face encounter with Jesus now, and not after death. If we can get to that place, do you realize how irrelevant death will become?

Did Moses or Aaron quarrel when they were told it was time to die? Did they seem fearful, afraid that their world was coming to an end? Maybe they understood something we don't. After all, isn't this the same Moses who appeared to Jesus on the Mount of Transfiguration? So, if someone told you today that they saw and spoke to Moses, how would you react?

I believe most people are content with the basic stuff. Christians are okay just being saved. In their minds, this whole idea of sonship is something they can begin to walk in when they die, and most people are fine with this.

I believe, even as the church, we function under a worldly system that has programmed our consciousness to keep us earthbound. So, the idea of being seated with Christ in heavenly places is just symbolism, not a reality. I have found that we have institutionalized and compartmentalized everything. We have also divided humanity into all kinds of categories, creating sects and divisions that were never a part of God's original plan. I have found that God's love is for humanity, not denominations, Christians, and all these separate categories that we fit people into. The principles established in the very beginning are all applicable to men, which is why it seems that the new agers have assumed ownership of stuff that belongs to all people. We think demons are so powerful without realizing that what they do is use human potential to further their agenda.

If we can see humanity from the perspective of "all people," our perceptions will begin to change. God is seeking to restore the breach and come into a right relationship with men, not ministers, pastors, Christians, and all these titles, and labels. For God so loved the WORLD—Are you getting this?

Absolutely nothing in your life will ever change without you changing. I find that we want change without changing. That is impossible. I also find that most Christians are not willing to abandon what they believe, even though they have no idea where their core beliefs came from. I also find that we prefer to create this fantasy world where we have convinced ourselves that something is working, or has value, when in truth, it is just a figment of our very real and active imaginations.

We are like our Father, so we have a natural ability to create the world that we live in, and we simultaneously blame others for the parts that don't seem to function the way they should. It is this fantasy world that must first be shattered before we can step into sonship. The good news is, it all gets shattered at death, and your immortal soul may have to be counseled to begin to understand the real world you find yourself in. The better news is that this shattering can be experienced while we live on earth. Only those who have walked this path have truly made the kind of impact on earth that the Father intended when He placed us here.

Most of us prefer to make excuses why we are 'less than.' When Jesus said if any man will come after Him, they must deny self, take up their cross and follow Him, He was not kidding. For us to live at the place of resurrection, we must first die with Christ. Paul talked about that, didn't he? It is death to self, to ego, that part of ourselves that was created to live and survive without God—it is our self-sufficiency, our self-preservation instinct, our innate ability to defend and justify ourselves—it is that part of us that must 'Die Daily.' It is the other you that fights against the real you.

I preach and teach, but realize that at the end of every message, the Word is still inside me because it has not found any ground to land on. I don't give information; I offer a more practical approach to change. Christianity was a label given to those who 'practiced the way of Christ.' It was never theoretical, or theological in nature, yet we place more emphasis on Christianity as theology than as a practice. You cannot walk with God theoretically or theologically. You have to practice. You have to implement. You have to 'do' what you 'hear.'

Let me give you an example. I spoke at my local church about the importance of taking communion, not just once a month, but daily, with family, with a spouse. If you study the scriptures carefully, you will see that is what the early church did. They never made a ritual out of it but practiced it whenever they met together. Many were moved by the message, and thought the Word was profound, as usual. Do you know how many applied this to their lives? Zero! I failed. Do you want to know why the church is not transforming? We love to be hearers of the Word only.

Paul thought he knew everything until he 'saw' Jesus. So did Abraham, Moses, Isaiah, Ezekiel, David, the Emissaries (Apostles), Mary Magdalene, and the list goes on and on. If new agers can leave their bodies and walk in the astral plane, why can't Christians leave their bodies and walk in the heavens? Isn't that what Jesus did? How do you think He 'saw what His Father was doing?' I believe human beings were created to live in both worlds simultaneously. Are you content with living a figurative, and assumed Christian life where you arbitrarily and randomly guess what is happening in the realm of the spirit? Most of the time you are wrong anyway! Don't you get concerned that 80% of your prayer life is ineffective? Or perhaps you prefer to live in fantasy land where it seems God's answer is mostly 'no' or 'wait.' My Bible says, "All

God's promises are yes and amen." (2 Corinthians 1:20)

Did you know that the Jews practice mystical Christianity? Even those who don't believe Jesus has come still practice mysticism. Even Jesus Himself said that "Salvation comes from the Jews" (see John 4:22). What do you think He meant by that?

The world and the church will start to change when you begin to change. You have to become the change you want to see. I love God's masterpiece called humanity. He made us a reflection of ourselves. The faults you see in others are faults you are identifying in yourself. If they weren't in you, it would be impossible to identify them in others. Let the change begin with you. You are more powerful than you think, especially when Holy Spirit lives inside you.

Prayer and Communion

Lord, help me not to be content with where I am on this journey. I know there is more. I know I must walk through the process to come into maturity. I know that faith is an action word and not a theology. Help me to practice and manifest my faith as Jesus did. Amen.

(Continue praying as the Spirit leads. You can pray in tongues, if you know how. Then take some time to just

sit quietly, eyes close, and listen. Silence your mind for a little while and approach the darkness you see without thought, and just listen. You may hear something, or you may not. When you are ready, open your eyes and take communion).

Lord, You said, as I eat and drink the flesh and blood of the Son of Man, I have life in me. Your flesh is real food and your blood is real drink. By eating your flesh and drinking your blood I enter into You and You into me. In the same way that the Father sent You here and You live because of Him, so when I make a meal of You, I will live because of You. You are the Bread from heaven. When I eat this Bread, I will live always.[17]

Lord, this is Your instruction to me. On the night of Your betrayal, you took bread. Having given thanks, You broke it and said, "This is my body, broken for you. Do this to remember me." After supper, You did the same thing with the cup: "This cup is my blood, my new covenant with you. Each time you drink this cup, remember me."

I declare that every time I eat this bread and drink this cup, I reenact in words and actions Your death, Lord. I will be drawn back to this meal again and again until

---

[17] see John 6:53-58 - MSG

You return. By faith, I eat Your body and drink Your blood.[18]

---

[18] see 1 Corinthians 11:24-28 - MSG

Day 10
Come Up Higher

On the day this was written, I fell asleep unexpectedly, and it was one of those afternoon naps where I lost total consciousness of this world, and found myself in another dimension. You do know that when you sleep, your soul/spirit leaves your body and go to explore, right? How else would you explain the phenomenon of dreams, and please don't always believe when the secular world attempts to define spiritual reality.

In the dream, I was at a particular place. It was familiar, and not familiar at the same time, but most of the people I know (family, church family, friends) were there. There was a very huge pool that people were taking off their clothes, and diving into. I found myself doing the same thing. The problem is, the pool of water was extremely polluted, but that did not stop us from having fun. The next thing I remember was a fight breaking out between two women that I know over a very familiar issue.

As I contemplated this dream, I found myself being upset yet again wondering why these are the places I go when I am asleep. There is always fighting, robbery, violence, and when there is water, it is always dirty. Water represents spirit in dreams. I started to seek for a deeper meaning to this reoccurrence, and I believe that is when Holy Spirit begun to speak.

That place was a lower realm, probably in the astral plane where there is corruption, fear, disharmony, but it is a familiar place—a comfort zone. We know very little of the dimensions that exist outside of this one. We are used to darkness, chaos, fighting, imperfections in the midst of fun. When we are together, we can ignore the filth in the world long enough to enjoy each other's company. After all, we are not convinced that we are responsible for the filth or that we can actually do something about it.

It was at this point that I was given this scripture:

Thus says the Lord: "Stand in the ways and see, and ask for the old paths, where the good way is, and walk in it; then you will find rest for your souls. but they said, 'We will not walk in it.'" (Jeremiah 6:16 - NKJV).

Some translations use the phrase "Ancient Paths" instead of "Old Paths." I found this interesting in lieu of my studies of Jewish Mysticism. The Jews interpret the Bible way different that we do in the western world.

We have naturalized spiritual things to our own detriment and have found ourselves wallowing in the muddied waters of the lower realm. But there is a path we are yet to set our feet on, an ancient path that the Jews know very well.

I believe we seldom know our true spiritual state because we really don't experience God through our senses. We don't believe in out of-body experiences, which means the scripture that says we are "seated with Christ in heavenly places" must be interpreted symbolically, and not as a living reality. Most of us don't even pay attention to our dreams, not realizing that those places we visit are more real than this physical world.

Let me paint a picture for you. Do you realize that when you dream, you are hardly conscious of this world? Do you realize that in your dream, you consciously live the experience as if it is a real one with no reference whatsoever to this world? Do you realize that if you died in your sleep, the new world you find yourself in would be like a dream with no end? Do you realize that when you dream you stand in creative light (which kind of looks like darkness that you can see in), and not necessarily light provided by the sun or moon? Our dreams point to a greater reality and should not be ignored.

I hear the Lord say, *"You have lived in the lower realms long enough. Come up higher. There is more. You pretend to know all when you know nothing. Open yourself up to be taught things you know nothing about. Be ready for new experiences you never thought possible. Rejoice when you find yourself with more questions than answers. It means you are getting it.*

Come higher. Ascend. There is an open invitation to come into My throne room boldly. Do it in your imagination, until it becomes real. Dream about it. Fantasize about it, until the desire awakens in you. Pray in the Spirit until you feel a shift within you to greater dimensions. This world is not all there is. This world is a mere dot in the wider reality of My kingdom. There are worlds to be explored; mandates to carry out; adventures to embark on. Come higher!"

Jeremiah 6:17 continues, **"Also I set watchmen over you, saying, Hearken to the sound of the trumpet."** I found this interesting because my mentor spoke about God setting up watchtowers; a people chosen by God not for fame or fortune, but to stop what is coming. I have seen for myself in scripture that a man in right relationship with God can change God's mind. I believe it. We have a much greater influence in the realm of the spirit than we realize, or are willing to believe, but if we continue to function in the lower dimensions, we will continue to do very little. The world is changing, and there is an open invitation for us to participate in that. Or we can continue to enjoy the murky waters of the lower dimensions, fighting demons and each other. As usual, the choice is yours.

Prayer and Communion

Lord, I have existed in the lower dimensions long enough. I am ready to take that leap of faith to come up higher. Like Peter, I will risk everything to take that step because You have called me to "Come." Help me to walk as Jesus walked, so I can do as Jesus did. Amen.

(Continue praying as the Spirit leads. You can pray in tongues, if you know how. Then take some time to just sit quietly, eyes close, and listen. Silence your mind for a little while and approach the darkness you see without thought, and just listen. You may hear something, or you may not. When you are ready, open your eyes and take communion).

Lord, You said, as I eat and drink the flesh and blood of the Son of Man, I have life in me. Your flesh is real food and your blood is real drink. By eating your flesh and drinking your blood I enter into You and You into me. In the same way that the Father sent You here and You live because of Him, so when I make a meal of

You, I will live because of You. You are the Bread from heaven. When I eat this Bread, I will live always.[19]

Lord, this is Your instruction to me. On the night of Your betrayal, you took bread. Having given thanks, You broke it and said, "This is my body, broken for you. Do this to remember me." After supper, You did the same thing with the cup: "This cup is my blood, my new covenant with you. Each time you drink this cup, remember me."

I declare that every time I eat this bread and drink this cup, I reenact in words and actions Your death, Lord. I will be drawn back to this meal again and again until You return. By faith, I eat Your body and drink Your blood.[20]

---

[19] see John 6:53-58 - MSG
[20] see 1 Corinthians 11:24-28 - MSG

Day 11
My Daily Prayer/Declarations

Today, I share a very special nugget for daily living and spiritual transcendence with you. These are not just words, but they speak to your identity in Christ; therefore, it is not just a prayer to be said, but who you become:

I decree and declare that my body is the temple of the Holy Spirit. I was fearfully and wonderfully made. I am the apple of God's eyes, His workmanship. I am co-heirs with Christ of the Kingdom of God. I am saved. I am justified by faith and sealed until that final day. I bear in my body the mark of Jesus Christ. I am salt and light on this earth. I am the head and not the tail. As Jesus is, so am I.

My Father is wealthy, and I am an heir of His estate. I walk in divine wealth. I walk in divine multiplication. I am fruitful, I multiply, and I am replenishing the earth. I walk in daily increase. I am debt-free; I will lend and not borrow. I give to the orphans and widows and sow my tithes on fertile ground. I am reaping according to God's Word. I am an embodiment of divine wealth.

I have the spirit of power, love, and sound mind. I have the mind of Christ. I think God-thoughts. I am an embodiment of perfect love. I think about what is lovely, pure, true, honest, of a good report. Where there is any virtue or praise, I think on those things. I am transformed by a renewed mind. I walk in power, love, and sound mind.

The fruit of the Spirit is evident in my life. I am healed by the stripes of Jesus. My soul is a new creation. I am born from above. I am seated with Christ in heavenly places. I have all spiritual blessings for life and godliness. I lack nothing. All things are mine. Nothing is impossible for me. I can do all things. Every organ and cell in my body is healthy. I have access to the broken body and shed blood of Jesus. I live in remembrance of what Jesus accomplished on my behalf. It is well with me.

I walk in the perpetual favor of God upon my life. I am blessed. When I go and when I come, I am blessed. I release the favor of God on the works on my hands. What I do will prosper. I make gold with the touch of my hands, and my breath. I am an embodiment of divinity. Christ in me, the hope of glory. As Jesus and the Father are one, so am I one with the Father. There is no separation between me and God. I perceive myself from a divine position. I live in union with God. I walk by faith, and it is accounted to me as righteousness. My borders are enlarging. I live and dwell under an open heaven. I am an embodiment of the name of God. What I decree is established in the heavens and on earth.

Prayer and Communion

Lord, may my declarations become my reality. You said I can decree and thing, and it will be established. You have called me to command the dawn, to speak to the day and bring my days to conform with Your will. May I understand the influence I have in creation. May my voice be recognized and responded to. Amen.

(Continue praying as the Spirit leads. You can pray in tongues, if you know how. Then take some time to just sit quietly, eyes close, and listen. Silence your mind for a little while and approach the darkness you see without thought, and just listen. You may hear something, or you may not. When you are ready, open your eyes and take communion).

Lord, You said, as I eat and drink the flesh and blood of the Son of Man, I have life in me. Your flesh is real food and your blood is real drink. By eating your flesh and drinking your blood I enter into You and You into me. In the same way that the Father sent You here and You live because of Him, so when I make a meal of

You, I will live because of You. You are the Bread from heaven. When I eat this Bread, I will live always. [21]

Lord, this is Your instruction to me. On the night of Your betrayal, you took bread. Having given thanks, You broke it and said, "This is my body, broken for you. Do this to remember me." After supper, You did the same thing with the cup: "This cup is my blood, my new covenant with you. Each time you drink this cup, remember me."

I declare that every time I eat this bread and drink this cup, I reenact in words and actions Your death, Lord. I will be drawn back to this meal again and again until You return. By faith, I eat Your body and drink Your blood. [22]

---

[21] see John 6:53-58 - MSG
[22] see 1 Corinthians 11:24-28 - MSG

Day 12
What Is Wrong With The Church

I have been in the church a long time, and I have learned and experienced a lot. But the most interesting era of my Christian journey started years ago when I was introduced to a paradigm I was not comfortable with; the supernatural move of God and the prophetic. I had never seen a lame man walk, a blind see or a dead raised back to life, and while I read about these things in the Bible, somehow I was convinced as everybody else was that this was no longer our reality. The Holy Spirit was a gift given so we can feel good and speak in another language, but we never learned to produce anything other than just babbling and running around the church and hitting each other over the head with a Bible. Yes, I experienced this for sitting and observing because, apparently, in a pentecostal movement, our lack of participation in the "crazy stuff" is a sure sign of being demon-possessed. Try sitting when everybody else is 'worshipping' and see how your day turns out.

Now, at the very foundation of our existence is this whole issue of opposition. We see this from the government all the way down to the church. Everybody is against everybody else, and one man is always trying to convince another that this is the right way, and you get labeled these days for disagreeing, especially if you disagree with someone who has a higher position than you do. I am not so sure when being right in our convictions was so intimately linked to our positions in church, but it can be uncomfortable for the layman. I have often asked God how He does it. How does He tolerate humanity when all we do is fight each other; speak death over each other; and sit in seats of judgment over one another. We dis-fellowship people from church because their sin is known and keep people in the pulpit who have mastered the art of hiding their own struggles with the very things others get dis-fellowshipped for, and we call this family. I started to think I had a higher probability of making it to heaven on my own, but that is just not God's design, unfortunately. So, I have to live with being labeled a rebel, disobedient, not flexible, deceived, etc.

The church is a messed-up place, with messed-up people who are always casting the blame on others for their own imperfections. What you judge and dislike in others is actually within you. You cannot judge another without judging yourself.

God made everything, including Adam and Eve, and put them in a garden with a tree He also made; the tree of the knowledge of good and evil. Every single human being has within them the potential for both good and evil.

Adam fell without having a conversation with the devil. He didn't even have a conversation with Eve. All he did was act on what was already in him. Give the devil a break, and go deal with your junk. Change yourself, and the world around you will change. Eve was deceived. Adam willfully disobeyed. Adam's act was greater because he was not deceived. Do you know what is deception? Deception is to be convinced via a conversation to act on your own evil inclinations. Adam acted on his own evil inclination without being deceived. You don't need the devil to disobey or reject God. You can do that all on your own.

The real journey of Christianity, regardless of your position in church, is to overcome the evil within you with good. Paul says it: **Do not be overcome by evil, but overcome evil with good. (Romans 12:21 – ESV).** This is not an external battle.

Oh, you thought he was talking about the devil.

He also says: **I do not understand what I do. For what I want to do I do not do, but what I hate I do. And if I do what I do not want to do, I agree that the law is good. As it is, it is no longer I myself who do it, but it is sin living in me. For I know that good** itself does not dwell in me, that is, in my sinful nature. For I have the desire to do what is good, but I cannot carry it out. For I do not do the good I want to do, but the evil I do not want to do—this I keep on doing. Now if I do what I do not want to do, it is no longer I who do it, but it is sin living in me that does it. So I find this law at work: Although I want to do good, evil is right there with me. For in my inner being I delight in God's law; but I see another law at work in me, waging war against the law of my mind and making me a prisoner of the law of sin at work within me. What a wretched man I am! Who will rescue me from this body that is subject to death? (Romans 7:15-24 – NIV).

We journey to get to that place where we can say, like Paul: **I have been crucified with Christ. It is no longer I who live, but Christ who lives in me. And the life I now live in the flesh I live by faith in the Son of God, who loved me and gave himself for me. (Galatians 2:20 – ESV).**

The problem with the church is everybody, and everybody thinking that everybody else is the problem. No, the problem with the church is YOU. Until all those "I" die and there is only Christ, there will always be problems.

On top of that, we have all created our own god in our own fallen image. That is why God sounds like us, acts like us, believes everything we believe; so nobody can convince us otherwise. We fit every new teaching into our old pattern of thinking. We may adjust it a little bit, reject what cannot fit, but we convince ourselves that we are into this new thing that God is doing, but we have not shifted in our actions, thoughts, beliefs, and perception. We force God to see life through our own eyes. Like, seriously. We have become our own gods, which is why we reject Him when He shows up as a donkey, a child, a prostitute, or anything else that makes us uncomfortable. God is God, not you.

So, I woke up thinking about Paul's words. I know we like to play god and sit in seats of judgment. The really gifted among us think it is their responsibility to weed out the sinners among us, so we expose each other's fault publicly and often speak against the people of God because they are doing things we don't agree with. This is not your job. God gave you one job; to love. So Paul says, I want to show you a more excellent way:

Though you can speak with the tongues of men and angels, and have the gift of prophecy whereby you understand all mysteries and knowledge...and even though you have the kind of faith to move every mountain but you do not have love, you are nothing. (1 Corinthians 13:1-3 – paraphrased).

The church is filled with gifted people, but it is also filled with broken and imperfect people. The church is also filled with judges, critics, gossipers, backbiters, hypocrites, and idol worshippers. I know, because I am one of them. I have abandoned my journey to please men because it is pointless and extremely exhausting trying to fit into their paradigm and serve their image of God. It took me a while to find God in all the mess, but now that I have seen just how different He is from us, I seek only to be like Him, to be conformed to His image. I am not different, and I have not changed for the worst; I am just waking up and that is my prayer for you today.

Prayer and Communion

Lord, I am tired of sleep-waking. I want to be intentional in walking with You throughout this journey. I know I am not from this world, but I am here, which means I have something to offer. I know I am not perfect, but that is not a pre-requisite to serving You. Help me to give my all in service to You, to leave this world, as Myles Monroe says, empty. Amen.

(Continue praying as the Spirit leads. You can pray in tongues, if you know how. Then take some time to just sit quietly, eyes close, and listen. Silence your mind for a little while and approach the darkness you see without thought, and just listen. You may hear

*something, or you may not. When you are ready, open
your eyes and take communion).*

Lord, You said, as I eat and drink the flesh and blood
of the Son of Man, I have life in me. Your flesh is real
food and your blood is real drink. By eating your flesh
and drinking your blood I enter into You and You into
me. In the same way that the Father sent You here and
You live because of Him, so when I make a meal of
You, I will live because of You. You are the Bread from
heaven. When I eat this Bread, I will live always.[23]

Lord, this is Your instruction to me. On the night of
Your betrayal, you took bread. Having given thanks,
You broke it and said, "This is my body, broken for
you. Do this to remember me." After supper, You did
the same thing with the cup: "This cup is my blood, my
new covenant with you. Each time you drink this cup,
remember me."

I declare that every time I eat this bread and drink this
cup, I reenact in words and actions Your death, Lord. I
will be drawn back to this meal again and again until
You return. By faith, I eat Your body and drink Your
blood.[24]

---

[23] see John 6:53-58 - MSG
[24] see 1 Corinthians 11:24-28 - MSG

Day 13
The Future Now

Time is an interesting concept when trying to understand it in the context of reality, but when there is an attempt to use time to measure or fathom eternity, it is then that we find great difficulty.

Time was created as a space in eternity, so it cannot be what we use to fathom the unfathomable. Likewise, there is great difficulty understanding the movements of our Creator in the context of time because He dwells in a realm outside of time, space, and matter, so these limitations do not apply to God.

Time never stands still, even when we do. So, time suggests that there is always movement. Time is divided into three segments: past, present, and future. The present moment is always moving further away from the past and closer to the future. The future appears static but malleable, seemingly changing certain events by the choices we make in the present.

When the future is brought into the past, it becomes the present. Therefore, we must learn to live from our true, positive future in order to establish the present moment we desire to experience. There is always more for us in the future; there is growth, development, maturity, knowledge, a greater version of ourselves that is ahead, but in the context of eternity, it is a now reality. This is why God can say to you that all things are yours, even though your present reality seems to contradict this. If you project a negative outcome and expectations into your future, then that will become your present.

Greater is He who is in you. We must always focus on bringing the future more here now. When we accept our present paradigm, thoughts, realities as standard, then we get trapped in a cycle where the present and past become a revolving reality that we tend to relive repeatedly, and future possibilities remain in the future, and it never manifests in our lives.

If you never partake of your future, you are actually stuck in the present moment, having the past consistently repeating itself until you die, and nothing ever changes. For change to occur, your future must become your present, so you must always look ahead with positivity, hope, faith; dream big, desire more, seek knowledge beyond what you know, engage with the unknown, and live from your future possibilities in the now.

Prayer and Communion

Lord, You said I already have all things for life and godliness. You said all things are mine; that I have inherited Your kingdom. You said I have all spiritual blessings in heavenly places. While I see all these possibilities in the future, I am struggling with accessing its reality now. So, my prayer today, is that You teach me how to access and live from my future while it is today. Amen.

(Continue praying as the Spirit leads. You can pray in tongues, if you know how. Then take some time to just sit quietly, eyes close, and listen. Silence your mind for a little while and approach the darkness you see without thought, and just listen. You may hear something, or you may not. When you are ready, open your eyes and take communion).

Lord, You said, as I eat and drink the flesh and blood of the Son of Man, I have life in me. Your flesh is real food and your blood is real drink. By eating your flesh and drinking your blood I enter into You and You into me. In the same way that the Father sent You here and You live because of Him, so when I make a meal of You, I will live because of You. You are the Bread from heaven. When I eat this Bread, I will live always.[25]

---

[25] see John 6:53-58 - MSG

Lord, this is Your instruction to me. On the night of Your betrayal, you took bread. Having given thanks, You broke it and said, "This is my body, broken for you. Do this to remember me." After supper, You did the same thing with the cup: "This cup is my blood, my new covenant with you. Each time you drink this cup, remember me."

I declare that every time I eat this bread and drink this cup, I reenact in words and actions Your death, Lord. I will be drawn back to this meal again and again until You return. By faith, I eat Your body and drink Your blood. [26]

---

[26] see 1 Corinthians 11:24-28 - MSG

Day 14
Do All Roads Lead To God?

I have always been an observer of reality from within and without. I have recently concluded that maybe having access to absolute earthly knowledge and cultures via the World Wide Web and ease of traveling may not be as enlightening as one would think it would be back in the day. And maybe it is, depending on the perspective from which it is viewed.

Every sect, people, ethnicity, or culture has formulated their own version of God, yet in close examination and scrutiny, maybe even experience, one has to wonder if the real God is anywhere to be found in all our different belief systems. One man says God created us in His image and likeness, and we have, in turn, returned the favor by creating Him in our image. But any God created in our image and chosen belief system will be mostly false because we are fundamentally flawed at the intrinsic human level by virtue of the fall. If we have no idea who we are in the fullness of God's original thought when He made man, then fundamentally, any idea we have of God will be equally flawed.

So now there are many gods, and the one who is seeking to find the real authentic God is faced with utter confusion or just plain ignorance as to how to carry out such pursuit.

Every culture has formed a version of God based on its "cultured" practices, rituals, and belief system. There is the God of the sabbath worshippers, the God of the Sunday worshippers (various versions), the God of the tongue speakers, the God of the no-tongue speakers, the prophetic God, the non-prophetic God, the God of 10% tithes, the God of 100% tithes, the God of no tithes, the God of genocide, the God of love, the God of hyper-grace, the God who wants to save a minority of human beings and send the rest to hell, the God of the Hindus, Buddhist, Jews, Gentiles, Jehovah's Witness, Mormons, Lodge; there is the harsh judge God, the very understanding God, the supernatural miracle-working God, the non-miracle-working God, the African God, the white man God, the black man God, the raise the dead God, the non-raise the dead God…. and this list is not even partially exhaustive.

No wonder some people believe there are many paths to God, and maybe this is true, but just not what we think it is. If there was a point in history where there was one God and one humanity, then the fragmentation we know today must be within the framework of humanity. Surely God is not fragmented, so there must

79

be a way for every sect of humanity to find their way back to God, even by the version of God they have concocted in their own culture.

Every fractured part of humanity believes in its exclusivity as if only by their way can we find God, but if this is true, then either everyone is right, or everyone is wrong.

I believe that Jesus is the way to the Father and the Bible is my rule of faith, even the parts I don't understand and struggle with, but to find our way to the Father, we must find our way to Jesus, and this is the responsibility of the breathe of God aka Holy Spirit. Surely then all belief systems must inevitably have a direct path to God and not away from Him, as we generally surmise, which provides some hope for the greater part of humanity that we would judge to be lost if we think our way is ultimately the only way to God.

The God we serve is usually framed by our preferred and chosen belief systems, which is influenced by our different cultures and life experiences and differ from person to person, and from church to church. The problem with this is, when God does a new thing, the old that we hold on to becomes an idol. The question is, why would God allow us to do that to Him unless He knows that ultimately our flawed perception of Him will ultimately lead us back to Him?

80

Food for thought.

Prayer and Communion

Lord, help me to have a right perspective of who You are and not be influenced by those who have created a version of You based solely on their life's experiences. You exist outside of time, and Your character is not shaped by what we go through on earth. May I approach You from this pure place, from an empty place, so I can experience who You truly are as You make Yourself known to me. Amen.

(Continue praying as the Spirit leads. You can pray in tongues, if you know how. Then take some time to just sit quietly, eyes close, and listen. Silence your mind for a little while and approach the darkness you see without thought, and just listen. You may hear something, or you may not. When you are ready, open your eyes and take communion).

Lord, You said, as I eat and drink the flesh and blood of the Son of Man, I have life in me. Your flesh is real food and your blood is real drink. By eating your flesh and drinking your blood I enter into You and You into me. In the same way that the Father sent You here and You live because of Him, so when I make a meal of

You, I will live because of You. You are the Bread from heaven. When I eat this Bread, I will live always.[27]

Lord, this is Your instruction to me. On the night of Your betrayal, you took bread. Having given thanks, You broke it and said, "This is my body, broken for you. Do this to remember me." After supper, You did the same thing with the cup: "This cup is my blood, my new covenant with you. Each time you drink this cup, remember me."

I declare that every time I eat this bread and drink this cup, I reenact in words and actions Your death, Lord. I will be drawn back to this meal again and again until You return. By faith, I eat Your body and drink Your blood.[28]

---

[27] see John 6:53-58 - MSG
[28] see 1 Corinthians 11:24-28 - MSG

Day 15
Oneness/Union With God

Union with God is spoken of by Jesus in His prayer recorded in John 17. The more I contemplate this subject, is the more insight and revelation I receive in my soul.

The enemy of union is separation. This wall we have erected between us and God is a perceived reality that is not real. There is no separation between the believer and God, but if we think and believe there is, then that becomes our reality. The downside to this perception or perceived wall of separation is our inability to manifest God on the earth; our inability to be effective stewards over the Father's estate.

Let's consider faith and the purpose of faith in the life of the believer. Is it just believing that God will do what we ask, think, or imagine, or does faith serve a much greater and divine purpose? I am leaning towards the latter. Faith is the technology we use to remove the projected wall of separation, so we can begin to comprehend, if possible, our oneness with God. Thus, partaking in the divine nature of God is only possible when we understand our union with the divine.

Why are we not seeing "more" manifested in the life of the believer? You cannot give what you do not have. As long as we think God has it and we don't, it becomes a challenge to manifest anything. Do you understand what it means to be co-heirs and joint heirs with Jesus? It means, what He has, we also have.

As long as the wall of separation remains, we will be limited in how much of God we can manifest on the earth. Only in union can there be a full manifestation of the sons of God; only in union can we do what God does; only in union can we say what God says. We are only able to give to the world what we have. This is what the disciples said:

But Peter said, "I don't have any silver or gold for you. But I'll give you what I have. In the name of Jesus Christ the Nazarene, get up and walk!" (Acts 3:6 – NLT).

They had the capacity to make the lame walk. Do you have it?

So I was having this internal dialogue with God, when I asked, "If union was present in man's original estate before the fall, why did God have to come down in the cool of the evening to commune with man?" Of course, this is what I was taught growing up in church.

I heard the Spirit of the Lord ask, "Who said God had to come down before the fall?"

As I revisited scripture, I realize that verse came after the fall because man was now out of alignment; he was not where he was supposed to be, so God came down asking, *"Where are you?"* Man was actually made to go "up." God had to come down because of the fall. Now that we are redeemed, we need to learn how to start going up again. *"Man, where are you? You were supposed to come up, but I didn't see you, so I had to come down looking for you. Where you at, Man?"*

If God is asking you that question right now, what is your response? The only true location for a child of God is "in Christ, in God, in His Name." Know your position and manifest God in a world that desperately needs Him.

Prayer and Communion

Lord, I see myself as one who dwells on the earth, but You also said I am seated with Christ in heavenly places. It means I am here and I am there. Help me to be conscious of where I am truly located so I can bring heaven to earth—"on earth as it is in heaven." Amen.

(Continue praying as the Spirit leads. You can pray in tongues, if you know how. Then take some time to just

sit quietly, eyes close, and listen. Silence your mind for a little while and approach the darkness you see without thought, and just listen. You may hear something, or you may not. When you are ready, open your eyes and take communion).

Lord, You said, as I eat and drink the flesh and blood of the Son of Man, I have life in me. Your flesh is real food and your blood is real drink. By eating your flesh and drinking your blood I enter into You and You into me. In the same way that the Father sent You here and You live because of Him, so when I make a meal of You, I will live because of You. You are the Bread from heaven. When I eat this Bread, I will live always.[29]

Lord, this is Your instruction to me. On the night of Your betrayal, you took bread. Having given thanks, You broke it and said, "This is my body, broken for you. Do this to remember me." After supper, You did the same thing with the cup: "This cup is my blood, my new covenant with you. Each time you drink this cup, remember me."

I declare that every time I eat this bread and drink this cup, I reenact in words and actions Your death, Lord. I will be drawn back to this meal again and again until

---

[29] see John 6:53-58 - MSG

You return. By faith, I eat Your body and drink Your blood.[30]

---

[30] see 1 Corinthians 11:24-28 - MSG

Day 16
You Are Born of God

I want to talk about you—your identity in Christ—who you are as a human being, especially as one who believes in Jesus Christ. Outside of Christ, you are still very special with great and unlimited potential, as you can see with all that humanity has accomplished to date.

But who are you in God? Let us talk about that. I have read the Bible from cover to cover twice, and I have drawn the conclusion that the Bible reveals humanity more than it reveals God. A book could not contain God anyway. As a matter of fact, we can only know God by what is seen, according to the Bible. And the thing that bears the most value in the 'seen realm' is humanity.

How can you hate your brother who you cannot see, and love God who you cannot see? It is impossible. So, God has revealed Himself to physical creation through humanity. Man is a revelation of God.

So, the Bible was written not so much for you to know God but for you to know who you are in God. The Bible is about you. It reveals who you are. It speaks to your identity. All the experiences the writers had can be yours. It speaks to what is possible.

You were God's idea. If He wanted to make a god-like being when He made you, who are you to argue? Why are we afraid to begin to embrace who we are? You are made in the image and likeness of God. You are born of God. You are God-born.

Here are some Scriptures that talk about you:

Genesis 1:26-28 (MSG) - God spoke: "Let us make human beings in our image, make them reflecting our nature so they can be responsible for the fish in the sea, the birds in the air, the cattle, and, yes, Earth itself, and every animal that moves on the face of Earth." God created human beings; he created them godlike, reflecting God's nature. He created them male and female. God blessed them: "Prosper! Reproduce! Fill Earth! Take charge! Be responsible for fish in the sea and birds in the air, for every living thing that moves on the face of Earth."

Genesis 5:24 (MSG) - Enoch walked steadily with God. And then one day he was simply gone: God took him.

2 Kings 2:11-14 (MSG) - And so it happened. They were walking along and talking. Suddenly a chariot

and horses of fire came between them and Elijah went up in a whirlwind to heaven. Elisha saw it all and shouted, "My father, my father! You—the chariot and cavalry of Israel!" When he could no longer see anything, he grabbed his robe and ripped it to pieces. Then he picked up Elijah's cloak that had fallen from him, returned to the shore of the Jordan, and stood there. He took Elijah's cloak—all that was left of Elijah!—and hit the river with it, saying, "Now where is the God of Elijah? Where is he?" When he struck the water, the river divided and Elisha walked through.

Exodus 33:17-19 (MSG) - God said to Moses: "All right. Just as you say; this also I will do, for I know you well and you are special to me. I know you by name." Moses said, "Please. Let me see your Glory." God said, "I will make my Goodness pass right in front of you; I'll call out the name, God, right before you. I'll treat well whomever I want to treat well and I'll be kind to whomever I want to be kind."

Psalm 8:4-8 (MSG) - I look up at your macro-skies, dark and enormous, your handmade sky-jewelry, moon and stars mounted in their settings. Then I look at my micro-self and wonder, why do you bother with us? Why take a second look our way? Yet we've so narrowly missed being gods, bright with Eden's dawn light. You put us in charge of your handcrafted world, repeated to us your Genesis-charge, made us lords of sheep and cattle, even animals out in the wild, birds flying and fish swimming, whales singing in the ocean deeps.

Mark 16:16-20 (MSG) - Then he said, "Go into the world. Go everywhere and announce the Message of God's good news to one and all. Whoever believes and is baptized is saved; whoever refuses to believe is damned. "These are some of the signs that will accompany believers: They will throw out demons in my name, they will speak in new tongues, they will take snakes in their hands, they will drink poison and not be hurt, they will lay hands on the sick and make them well." Then the Master Jesus, after briefing them, was taken up to heaven, and he sat down beside God in the place of honor. And the disciples went everywhere preaching, the Master working right with them, validating the Message with indisputable evidence.

Need I say more?

Prayer and Communion

Lord, what does it mean that I am born again? Help me to understand. You said I am a new creation; old things have passed, and all things have become new. Lord, what does this mean? What are Your thoughts towards me? What is my assignment? What would You have me do this day? Amen.

(Continue praying as the Spirit leads. You can pray in tongues, if you know how. Then take some time to just sit quietly, eyes close, and listen. Silence your mind for a little while and approach the darkness you see without thought, and just listen. You may hear something, or you may not. When you are ready, open your eyes and take communion).

Lord, You said, as I eat and drink the flesh and blood of the Son of Man, I have life in me. Your flesh is real food and your blood is real drink. By eating your flesh and drinking your blood I enter into You and You into me. In the same way that the Father sent You here and You live because of Him, so when I make a meal of You, I will live because of You. You are the Bread from heaven. When I eat this Bread, I will live always.[31]

Lord, this is Your instruction to me. On the night of Your betrayal, you took bread. Having given thanks, You broke it and said, "This is my body, broken for you. Do this to remember me." After supper, You did the same thing with the cup: "This cup is my blood, my new covenant with you. Each time you drink this cup, remember me."

---

[31] see John 6:53-58 - MSG

I declare that every time I eat this bread and drink this cup, I reenact in words and actions Your death, Lord. I will be drawn back to this meal again and again until You return. By faith, I eat Your body and drink Your blood.[32]

---

[32] see 1 Corinthians 11:24-28 - MSG

Day 17
Who Is The God Of This World?

I will start this conversation, but I will leave it open for you to do your own research and draw your own conclusions.

I held on to this revelation for a very long time because I was unsure of the timing of releasing it. But as I continued to observe the world, in tears, I have seen what Christianity has become. For me, it is a sad reality because, as a student of the Word of God and having studied and followed some Christian mystics of our day, I know what Christianity can be. I am sure what it is predominantly now is not what Jesus intended when He established the church on His own broken body and spilled blood.

We were given a tool to transform the world and usher in the manifested glory of God. Instead, we used it to serve our own whims and fantasies, to elevate ourselves to places of prominence and power, and made it about money. I finally know what is fundamentally wrong with Christianity. It is the ego we serve thinking it is the true and living God. Which also suggest that the ego a.k.a. false self is more the god of this world than the devil.

I know Jesus de-powered the devil by His death, burial, resurrection, and ascension, so I have been trying to figure out who is the god of this world that blinds the minds of people to the truth. At first, I thought it was money because Jesus made a profound statement by claiming we cannot serve two masters; we cannot serve God and money. The love of money seemed to be at the root of society's functionality so I thought mammon must definitely be the god of this world.

Lo and behold, another god revealed itself just recently with the current trends.

Now the ego is a false self, and it will not exist beyond our physical death. It is the ego that does not want to die; the ego that Paul referenced when he said, "I die daily." The ego is the "I" that interjects itself in areas of influence in our lives, often parading in the dark as the "voice of God," unbeknownst to us who follow its promptings blindly and without question.

The ego is of our own creation, which means its destruction must come by our own hands.

The ego demands to be right; it wants to be served and submitted to; obeyed and worshiped and given seats of prominence, special treatment, and always demands special recognition. Why is it so demanding, so hungry for attention? It does not want to die. In death, the ego ceases to exist, and it knows it has no eternal inheritance. It wants you to live so it can thrive and rule.

The whole purpose of going through difficulties and trauma is a process to try and dissolve the ego to destroy it and render it powerless.

The ego will keep us in fear as a survival mechanism. It does not want to be discovered, so it camouflages itself as God with Biblical backing, but it does not want to die, for this is the only opportunity it gets at existing.

The ego is powerful. It is the you that wants to be but is not. If the ego cannot die, it must be denied.

Prayer and Communion

Lord, so many times I am controlled by the ego that seeks to usurp Your authority and rule my life. Its voice often lead me astray and causes me to respond to circumstances in an ungodly manner. Fighting it may seem like a hopeless venture, but You have given me authority over everything that would oppose You. I want Your voice to be the dominant voice in my life. Teach me to hear and obey only You. Teach me to die to self; that You may live through me. Amen.

(Continue praying as the Spirit leads. You can pray in tongues, if you know how. Then take some time to just sit quietly, eyes close, and listen. Silence your mind for a little while and approach the darkness you see without thought, and just listen. You may hear something, or you may not. When you are ready, open your eyes and take communion).

Lord, You said, as I eat and drink the flesh and blood of the Son of Man, I have life in me. Your flesh is real food and your blood is real drink. By eating your flesh and drinking your blood I enter into You and You into me. In the same way that the Father sent You here and You live because of Him, so when I make a meal of You, I will live because of You. You are the Bread from heaven. When I eat this Bread, I will live always. [33]

Lord, this is Your instruction to me. On the night of Your betrayal, you took bread. Having given thanks, You broke it and said, "This is my body, broken for you. Do this to remember me." After supper, You did the same thing with the cup: "This cup is my blood, my new covenant with you. Each time you drink this cup, remember me."

I declare that every time I eat this bread and drink this cup, I reenact in words and actions Your death, Lord. I

---

[33] see John 6:53-58 - MSG

will be drawn back to this meal again and again until You return. By faith, I eat Your body and drink Your blood.[34]

---

[34] see 1 Corinthians 11:24-28 - MSG

Day 18
As He Is, So Are We

The Word of God really doesn't mince words when it comes to our identity. The knowledge of who we are in God is beyond articulation. We are literally afraid to say it because it sounds wrong, so we try to develop a "safe" language where we are able to digress certain knowledge and process it without feeling like we are overstepping our bounds.

What I will say is that who we are was always God's idea, not ours. If He is comfortable thinking of us in a certain light, then we must, at the very least, try to develop a language and an understanding of such a reality, if we are ever going to accomplish the mandate given to man at the beginning of time.

Take this short journey with me…Jesus is made heir of "all things." It was through Jesus that the world was made.

Some translations use "ages" in place of "worlds." Ages speak to what has passed, what age we are now in and the ages to come, so the past, present, and future are all reconciled in the person of Jesus Christ.

Jesus is the radiance of God's glory; the exact representation of God's nature; upholds all things by the Word of His power.

Jesus is much better than the angels by virtue of His inheritance as the Son of God.

I like to connect the first Adam before the fall to the second Adam who knew no sin, though experienced the same temptations we do. I like to see both as the full embodiment of what a human being was made to be, and function. I draw from that as the standard to which we should aim for and pursue relentlessly. Man cannot be known as man is now, and to embrace this as our true selves would be a great travesty in the broader consideration of what was in the mind of God when He said, "Let Us make man."

The Bible did say: **By this is love perfected with us, so that we may have confidence for the day of judgment, because as he is so also are we in this world. (1 John 4:17 – ESV).**

It is hard to fathom the "oneness reality" with such imperfect beings as us. We think we are not worthy to be in union with Christ, but that was God's idea too, not ours. We struggle with the idea because we think to entertain such things is pulling God down to our level, and maybe He did come down to our level and allow

Himself to walk the path of a fallen human in the name of redemption, but why? If the value of something is measured by what one is willing to pay for it, then a human life is worth the sacrifice of divinity, which can only suggest that God knows something about us that we don't yet know.

Just in case there is a temptation to cross over into arrogance, thinking oneness with God is parallel to equality, I will remind you of what the mystics say: *"He is our essence, but we are not His."*

Prayer and Communion

Lord, You prayed in John 17 that we would be one with You as You are one with the Father. I now embrace this oneness, though I do not understand or comprehend such a reality. I declare that I am in You, and You are in me. I know You are as close to me as the air I breathe. Help me to live in full awareness and consciousness of the fact that You will never leave or forsake me because I am one with You, and nothing can separate me from You. Amen.

(Continue praying as the Spirit leads. You can pray in tongues, if you know how. Then take some time to just sit quietly, eyes close, and listen. Silence your mind for a little while and approach the darkness you see without thought, and just listen. You may hear

101

something, or you may not. When you are ready, open your eyes and take communion).

Lord, You said, as I eat and drink the flesh and blood of the Son of Man, I have life in me. Your flesh is real food and your blood is real drink. By eating your flesh and drinking your blood I enter into You and You into me. In the same way that the Father sent You here and You live because of Him, so when I make a meal of You, I will live because of You. You are the Bread from heaven. When I eat this Bread, I will live always.[35]

Lord, this is Your instruction to me. On the night of Your betrayal, you took bread. Having given thanks, You broke it and said, "This is my body, broken for you. Do this to remember me." After supper, You did the same thing with the cup: "This cup is my blood, my new covenant with you. Each time you drink this cup, remember me."

I declare that every time I eat this bread and drink this cup, I reenact in words and actions Your death, Lord. I will be drawn back to this meal again and again until You return. By faith, I eat Your body and drink Your blood.[36]

---

[35] see John 6:53-58 - MSG
[36] see 1 Corinthians 11:24-28 - MSG

Day 19
Maturing and Unity of the Body of Christ (the Church)

There are things that need to be established for the body of Christ (church) to come into perfection (maturity) and unity. Be mindful that unity does not speak to everyone believing the same thing, but there must be unity in diversity. I believe a misconception and misinterpretation of what "unity" is has caused the church to get stuck in infancy. If we are going to "grow up into the Head," we need to understand and establish some divine principles and offices in our church structure.

What we need fully manifested in us are:

- The seven Spirits of God.
- The five-fold ministry.
- The gifts of the Spirit.
- The fruit of the Spirit.

Let's quote the Scriptures:

The Spirit of the Lord shall rest upon Him, the Spirit of wisdom and understanding, the Spirit of

counsel and might, the Spirit of knowledge and of the fear of the Lord. (Isaiah 11:2 – NKJV).

John to the seven churches that are in Asia: Grace to you and peace from him who is and who was and who is to come, and from the seven spirits who are before his throne. (Revelation 1:4 – ESV).

"And to the angel of the church in Sardis write: 'The words of him who has the seven spirits of God and the seven stars. 'I know your works. You have the reputation of being alive, but you are dead.'" (Revelation 3:1 – ESV).

From the throne came flashes of lightning, and rumblings and peals of thunder, and before the throne were burning seven torches of fire, which are the seven spirits of God. (Revelation 4:5 – ESV).

And between the throne and the four living creatures and among the elders I saw a Lamb standing, as though it had been slain, with seven horns and with seven eyes, which are the seven spirits of God sent out into all the earth. (Revelation 5:6 – ESV).

We don't talk much about the seven spirits of God in church circles, but they are given to the church for the building up of the body of Christ. To some extent, we function minimally in some of the attributes of these spirits but not in its fullest manifestation because our knowledge about them is limited.

And He Himself gave some to be apostles, some prophets, some evangelists, and some pastors and teachers, for the equipping of the saints for the work of ministry, for the edifying of the body of Christ, till we all come to the unity of the faith and of the knowledge of the Son of God, to a perfect man, to the measure of the stature of the fullness of Christ; that we should no longer be children, tossed to and fro and carried about with every wind of doctrine, by the trickery of men, in the cunning craftiness of deceitful plotting, but, speaking the truth in love, may grow up in all things into Him who is the head—Christ— (Ephesians 4:11-15 – NKJV).

If we look at this in context, unless the five-fold is fully established in our churches, we will be tossed to and fro with every wind of doctrine by the trickery of men.

Many believers depend more on other people's interpretation of Scripture than on what the Holy Spirit within may be revealing to them. Our belief system must not be shaped by other people's opinions. What others have to say must be given due consideration in light of our own personal journey with the Lord, what the Holy Spirit is revealing to us, and Scripture.

If the apostolic and the prophetic ministry is missing from our churches, then there is no correction for bad doctrine, and no spiritual alignment when things are out of whack, and this is what we see happening in most churches.

But the manifestation of the Spirit is given to each one for the profit of all: for to one is given the word of wisdom through the Spirit, to another the word of knowledge through the same Spirit, to another faith by the same Spirit, to another gifts of healings by the same Spirit, to another the working of miracles, to another prophecy, to another discerning of spirits, to another different kinds of tongues, to another the interpretation of tongues. But one and the same Spirit works all these things, distributing to each one individually as He wills. (1 Corinthians 12:7-11 - NKJV).

For I say, through the grace given to me, to everyone who is among you, not to think of himself more highly than he ought to think, but to think soberly, as God has dealt to each one a measure of faith. For as we have many members in one body, but all the members do not have the same function, so we, being many, are one body in Christ, and individually members of one another. Having then gifts differing according to the grace that is given to us, let us use them: if prophecy, let us prophesy in

proportion to our faith; or ministry, let us use it in our ministering; he who teaches, in teaching; he who exhorts, in exhortation; he who gives, with liberality; he who leads, with diligence; he who shows mercy, with cheerfulness. (Romans 12:3-8 – NKJV).

But the fruit of the Spirit is love, joy, peace, longsuffering, kindness, goodness, faithfulness, gentleness, self-control. Against such there is no law. (Galatians 5:22-23 – NKJV).

This text in Galatians is worded funny because fruit is not pluralized, suggesting there is just one fruit.

These must be studied, implemented, developed through practice, established, and allowed to function freely within each believer for the full benefit of the body of Christ. There is no unity if one part is missing. There can be no maturation or coming into perfection without these.

I have been a silent observer of the church for years, and I am now more convinced that these are necessary for the building up of the body of Christ, and no amount of theology we create to counteract the necessity for these will be of any lasting benefit to us.

Prayer and Communion

Lord, I know I have access to the seven spirits of God, and I should be operating in the gifts of the Spirit and manifesting the fruit of the Spirit. I feel like I have been measured and found wanting. I will no more ignore the reality of the necessity for these to be functioning in me and the body of Christ. May You activate what You have deposited in me, so I can manifest Your will and power on earth. Teach me Your ways so I may walk in them. Amen.

(Continue praying as the Spirit leads. You can pray in tongues, if you know how. Then take some time to just sit quietly, eyes close, and listen. Silence your mind for a little while and approach the darkness you see without thought, and just listen. You may hear something, or you may not. When you are ready, open your eyes and take communion).

Lord, You said, as I eat and drink the flesh and blood of the Son of Man, I have life in me. Your flesh is real food and your blood is real drink. By eating your flesh and drinking your blood I enter into You and You into me. In the same way that the Father sent You here and You live because of Him, so when I make a meal of

You, I will live because of You. You are the Bread from heaven. When I eat this Bread, I will live always.[37]

Lord, this is Your instruction to me. On the night of Your betrayal, you took bread. Having given thanks, You broke it and said, "This is my body, broken for you. Do this to remember me." After supper, You did the same thing with the cup: "This cup is my blood, my new covenant with you. Each time you drink this cup, remember me."

I declare that every time I eat this bread and drink this cup, I reenact in words and actions Your death, Lord. I will be drawn back to this meal again and again until You return. By faith, I eat Your body and drink Your blood.[38]

---

[37] see John 6:53-58 - MSG
[38] see 1 Corinthians 11:24-28 - MSG

Day 20
Have We Made Christianity Into A Cult?

Please read with an open mind and keen understanding, considering prayerfully the perspective from which I write. This is not an attack on the church but an evaluation of what it is; caution perhaps, and maybe identifying some measure of correcting that we need to do. According to Isaiah, we are called to be repairers of the breach. The original mandate given to man included replenishing the earth. This means where resources are running out, we have the capacity to refill it. This also means where there is error, we have the power to correct it.

The word cult is derived from the word "culture." Culture is defined as "the ideas, customs, and social behaviour of a particular people or society." Many times I have asked why the church here in Jamaica seems so different from the churches overseas and was told it is a matter of culture. This is not a very good answer, considering what the word means.

Cult is defined as: *a system of religious veneration and devotion directed towards a particular figure or object;*

a relatively small group of people having religious beliefs or practices regarded by others as strange or as imposing excessive control over members; a misplaced or excessive admiration for a particular thing.

The Bible says where the Spirit of the Lord is, there is liberty (See 2 Corinthians 3:17). John 8:36 says, **"Therefore if the Son makes you free, you shall be free indeed."** So believers in Christ should be the truly free human beings walking on this earth, yet we seem to enter into some level of bondage and control when we become saved. The Bible is clear that our faith in God and the Lord Jesus Christ is not about a day, food, dress code, or even living by the law.

Who has made us sufficient to be ministers of a new covenant, not of the letter but of the Spirit. For the letter kills, but the Spirit gives life. (2 Corinthians 3:6 – ESV).

Christianity is a walk with the Spirit and coming into union with God, as demonstrated by the example Jesus set for us. He did not only purchase our freedom, but opened up an ancient path that we can once again have true fellowship with our Father and Creator, and with each other. This is true liberty, but this is not what Christianity is all about, now is it? Or maybe I should specifically say "church."

My personal experience with church has been a bitter one. I experienced some people seemingly from my denomination totally turn against me and even try to poison the minds of those who stand by me. Why? Because I choose to believe differently. I choose to question everything. I choose to let go of even some doctrines that are not Biblical. I choose to interpret scripture from a mystical/spiritual perspective. I choose to interpret Scripture from the perspective of 'God is love,' and human beings are very valuable to Him, because we were made in His image and likeness. For some reason, it seems like we want to believe that human beings are nothing but worms and wretches, and I no longer believe that.

So, I was invited to a Facebook group that I don't quite fit in, but I joined out of curiosity. It has hundreds of members and is centered around the idea of overcoming trauma from religion, particularly Christianity. I have been privy to hear hundreds of stories from people who are walking away from Christianity (more so church) because of the years of mental bondage and abuse (mentally, verbally, physically) that they had to endure.

There are people who hold fast to what is termed "sound doctrine" who are physically abusive to their spouse and children, adulterers, fornicators, liars and homosexuals. They live a very fragmented life and force those connected to them to believe the same thing they believe or suffer the consequences. Some of these people hold leadership positions in the church. From what I know about church (having grown up in church), this is predominantly how we function: We put great emphasis on punishing sin, disfellowshipping those who make mistakes, stripping them of responsibilities, and extending great judgment that sometimes extend beyond the four walls of the church. My self-worth, self-esteem, self-confidence, and the value I put on myself was totally diminished, in some instances, eradicated by church. Many, many people remain in churches only because of their genuine love for God, and because they have been forced to think that walking away from church is walking away from God.

The church is supposed to be an organism made up of members of the body of Christ, which means the people are the church, and a member of a body cannot cease to be a member, even if they are not functioning according to the call and gifting on their lives. The body actually suffers from a dysfunctional member. If we make the church into an institution, with a religious-based structure with rules (dos and don'ts) and guidelines and laws about what to believe, how to act, how to dress, what to eat, which day to worship, when to worship, how to worship, and the host of ideas we are forced to conform to in order to be accepted within that particular movement, and we make this priority over people, then we are a cult.

Yes, the court system has rules and laws and a particular order that must be conformed to, and all other systems of the world do as well. As Christians, if we are operating within any of these systems, it is recommended that we conform or suffer any consequences, but these are systems of the world that we live in, so it is advised that we adhere to those laws in order to avoid any consequences that may arise from that. The church was not meant to function under the same system or with the same expectations as the systems of this world. We are from another world, and our citizenship is from a happy and liberated place outside of creation.

Christianity is supposed to be a Spirit-led life. The Spirit-led life is just that, Spirit-led, and it is not necessarily built on a hierarchy. We need leaders who know how to facilitate growth and lead with enough room for individuals to explore their personal journey with the Holy Spirit within them. Yes, we will make a lot of mistakes, but a part of life and growth is learning from our mistakes.

As members, we don't all have the same function. Samson was called to be a Nazarite, so God specifically told him not to cut his hair or drink alcohol. Another may be called to the marketplace, so it is necessary to be well-groomed and well-dressed. Someone else may be called to the inner city, so locking their hair, tattoos and piercings may enhance their witness capabilities. By the way, the word *witnessing* in this context has to do with demonstrating the power of the Holy Spirit so unbelievers know that God is real. The true gospel was never about warning people about hell. You become a witness because you have seen what God can do, and you do likewise.

The church of the future must address these issues or run the risk of becoming irrelevant in a world saturated with divine knowledge.

Prayer and Communion

Lord, I am seeking to know my place in Your kingdom. I believe You have called me to more than just being a member of an institution. We so often follow rules at the expense of an authentic relationship with You. I choose to be led by Your Spirit because You said only those who are led by Your Spirit are truly Your children. I don't want to hear at the end of my sojourn here on earth "I know You not." Speak, Lord, Your servant is listening. Amen.

(Continue praying as the Spirit leads. You can pray in tongues, if you know how. Then take some time to just

sit quietly, eyes close, and listen. Silence your mind for a little while and approach the darkness you see without thought, and just listen. You may hear something, or you may not. When you are ready, open your eyes and take communion).

Lord, You said, as I eat and drink the flesh and blood of the Son of Man, I have life in me. Your flesh is real food and your blood is real drink. By eating your flesh and drinking your blood I enter into You and You into me. In the same way that the Father sent You here and You live because of Him, so when I make a meal of You, I will live because of You. You are the Bread from heaven. When I eat this Bread, I will live always.[39]

Lord, this is Your instruction to me. On the night of Your betrayal, you took bread. Having given thanks, You broke it and said, "This is my body, broken for you. Do this to remember me." After supper, You did the same thing with the cup: "This cup is my blood, my new covenant with you. Each time you drink this cup, remember me."

I declare that every time I eat this bread and drink this cup, I reenact in words and actions Your death, Lord. I will be drawn back to this meal again and again until

---

[39] see John 6:53-58 - MSG

You return. By faith, I eat Your body and drink Your blood.[40]

---

[40] see 1 Corinthians 11:24-28 - MSG

Day 21
Tasted of the Good Word of God

For the word of God is living and active and sharper than any two-edged sword, and piercing as far as the division of soul and spirit, of both joints and marrow, and able to judge the thoughts and intentions of the heart. (Hebrews 4:12 – NASB).

I think we do the "Word of God" a great injustice by limiting Him to only a book, when He is so much more. Jesus is the Word who became flesh and dwelt among us (See John 1:14). There is no disputing this as fact:

God, after He spoke long ago to the fathers in the prophets in many portions and in many ways, in these last days has spoken to us in His Son, whom He appointed heir of all things, through whom also He made the world. (Hebrews 1:1-2 – NASB).

But there is something we may have missed in how we interpret the Scriptures because it was Jesus, the Word made flesh, who said:

It is written, 'Man shall not live on bread alone, but on every word that proceeds out of the mouth of God.'" (Matthew 4:4 – NASB).

Jesus was quoting a Scripture from Deuteronomy, and this reference to the Word was not about the Bible. The Bible does not contain all the Words spoken by God, and every mention of the "Word of God" in Scripture was spoken before there was a Bible. The correction here is not to idolize the Bible and make it God. We need to see the Bible's importance in its proper context.

In the beginning was the Word, and the Word was with God, and the Word was God. (John 1:1 – NASB).

This text speaks to three different levels of the Word converging into One Person. The Word of God is a spiritual entity in which we live, move, breathe, and have our existence. The reality is, the world and everything in it are held together by the vibrational frequency of the voice of God, which means His voice reverberates throughout creation and holds everything together. If God should stop speaking for a milli-second, the world and everything in it would disappear and cease to exist. It is true that God is God all by Himself. It is only by His voice can anything else exist.

From a scientific perspective, the human body is made up of 37.2 trillion cells. If you pull these cells apart, the body will disappear because the cells are not visible to the human eye. What science cannot definitively say is what holds these cells together. I believe the answer is "the Word of God."

The Bible speaks of the Word of God as a living entity:

- the Word of God came to Nathan (see 1 Chronicles 17:3).
- the Word of God increased (see Acts 6:7).
- the Word of God grew and multiplied (see Acts 12:24).
- the Word of God grew mightily and prevailed (see Acts 19:20).
- the Word of God is quick, and powerful and sharper than any two-edged sword (see Hebrews 4:12).
- the Word of God liveth and abideth forever (see 1 Peter 1:23).
- His name is called the Word of God (see Revelation 19:13).

The Word of God is tangible and can be seen. Proverbs 30:5 refers to the Word of God as "he." The Word of God is also referred to as a seed, which means it can produce something.

We are commissioned to eat the good Word of God and live an abundant life. This is more than just reading the Bible. This is also communion. God has always desired for us to encounter and experience Him. The Bible was written to help us know when it is Him that we are experiencing. There are other beings that come into the earth pretending to be God.

We must see the Word of God as more than just a book. We grossly limit God, and ourselves, by doing this. If you are reading this, and you have gotten thus far in this journey, I want to believe that God is removing any mental limitations you may have in order to reposition you so He can reveal Himself to you as He truly is.

Get ready!

Prayer and Communion

Lord, as I open myself up to receiving divine downloads from the written Word of God, may You also position me to have encounters with the living Word of God. Help me be ready for my hour of visitation. Amen.

(Continue praying as the Spirit leads. You can pray in tongues, if you know how. Then take some time to just sit quietly, eyes close, and listen. Silence your mind for a little while and approach the darkness you see

without thought, and just listen. You may hear something, or you may not. When you are ready, open your eyes and take communion).

Lord, You said, as I eat and drink the flesh and blood of the Son of Man, I have life in me. Your flesh is real food and your blood is real drink. By eating your flesh and drinking your blood I enter into You and You into me. In the same way that the Father sent You here and You live because of Him, so when I make a meal of You, I will live because of You. You are the Bread from heaven. When I eat this Bread, I will live always.[41]

Lord, this is Your instruction to me. On the night of Your betrayal, you took bread. Having given thanks, You broke it and said, "This is my body, broken for you. Do this to remember me." After supper, You did the same thing with the cup: "This cup is my blood, my new covenant with you. Each time you drink this cup, remember me."

I declare that every time I eat this bread and drink this cup, I reenact in words and actions Your death, Lord. I will be drawn back to this meal again and again until You return. By faith, I eat Your body and drink Your blood.[42]

---

[41] see John 6:53-58 - MSG
[42] see 1 Corinthians 11:24-28 - MSG

Day 22
The Lord's Day is the Last Day

There is only one mention of the Lord's Day in Scripture:

"I was in the Spirit on the Lord's day, and heard behind me a great voice, as of a trumpet." (Revelation 1:10 – KJV).

Note that John said he was "in the Spirit" which can be equated to Paul's exhortation to "Walk in the Spirit" (see Galatians 5:16). He was in the Spirit on the Lord's day, which we often call a vision. Those who do not believe in the spiritual realm put very little value on visions. They will say "it's all in your head." We would be surprised at how much of reality is really in "our heads."

This one reference on the Lord's day led to a search for what is really meant by the last days, considering that most of Christendom tends to have this perception, especially when there is chaos and global disharmony, that the world is ending. I notice that Jesus referred to the "last day" several times (See John 6:40, John 6:44, John 6:54, John 12:48). But then all the other Biblical writers added an "s" to day, making it plural (See Acts 2:17, 2 Timothy 3:1, Hebrews 1:2, James 5:3 and 2 Peter 3:3). The mistake I think we make is to measure God's timing by the days of the week, even knowing these were established on pagan principles and named after pagan gods.

In Genesis, there was the evening and the morning that constituted a day, even before the sun, moon, and stars came into existence. Even then, I am sure time did not progress as it does after the fall of man, because everything changed when man fell. So I am thinking that the Lord's Day either began in the beginning of time or it began after His death, burial, resurrection and ascension. It is "His Day" and another word used in Scripture is "Now."

"Now faith is the substance of things hoped for, the evidence of things not seen." (Hebrews 11:1).

"For he saith, I have heard thee in a time accepted, and in the day of salvation have I succoured thee: behold, now is the accepted time; behold, now is the day of salvation." (2 Corinthians 6:2).

My conclusion: the Lord's Day is also the Last Day, not days. This day, which is called "now" is a perpetual day that is constituted by changes in era or ages, where one age ends and another begin, but this day has an end when time as we know it will be no more. Some call it the restoration of all things; some say it is the consummation of the marriage between Jesus and His bride; I believe it is a glorious day when Jesus **"present the church to himself in splendor, without spot or wrinkle or anything like that, but holy and blameless." (Ephesians 5:27 – CSB).**

Every Christian knows intuitively when an era is ending for a new one to begin, but it is usually perceived as the end of the world. I wish we would change our perception and realize that there is a reason we are still here. Even if the world was ending, we should petition the Father by virtue of what we know He wants to accomplish in creation that our task is not yet completed. Many Christians have not even begun to walk in their divine call and purpose because they are distracted by ignorance, entertainment, the pursuit of the lust of the eyes, the blunders and imperfection of others, and a whole list of things designed to take our eyes off the prize.

We are living in the Lord's Day on the Last Day, and we need to be focused on what we are called to do. I am begging leaders of churches and ministries to release their members so they can fully embrace the call that is on their lives. No leader wants to stand before God to give an account for being a hindrance to those who were called to the kingdom of God for a specific purpose.

Prayer and Communion

Lord, You are the Lord of all ages. As time passes by, and ages change and generations change, with the increase in knowledge and technology, You remain unchanging and always faithful to Your promises. This is Your day, Your time, and maybe it is the Last Day, but help me not to focus on chaos but on the glory that will cover the earth as the waters cover the sea. May I have a right perspective of reality and see the world as You see it. Amen.

(Continue praying as the Spirit leads. You can pray in tongues, if you know how. Then take some time to just sit quietly, eyes close, and listen. Silence your mind for a little while and approach the darkness you see without thought, and just listen. You may hear something, or you may not. When you are ready, open your eyes and take communion).

Lord, You said, as I eat and drink the flesh and blood of the Son of Man, I have life in me. Your flesh is real food and your blood is real drink. By eating your flesh and drinking your blood I enter into You and You into me. In the same way that the Father sent You here and You live because of Him, so when I make a meal of

You, I will live because of You. You are the Bread from heaven. When I eat this Bread, I will live always. [43]

Lord, this is Your instruction to me. On the night of Your betrayal, you took bread. Having given thanks, You broke it and said, "This is my body, broken for you. Do this to remember me." After supper, You did the same thing with the cup: "This cup is my blood, my new covenant with you. Each time you drink this cup, remember me."

I declare that every time I eat this bread and drink this cup, I reenact in words and actions Your death, Lord. I will be drawn back to this meal again and again until You return. By faith, I eat Your body and drink Your blood. [44]

---

[43] see John 6:53-58 - MSG
[44] see 1 Corinthians 11:24-28 - MSG

Day 23
Divine Purpose and Destiny

In the last few decades, great emphasis has been placed on finding one's divine purpose and destiny. It is a search to answer the age-old questions, "Why am I here? What is the purpose of life? Is there more?" This has been my personal journey now for almost a decade. Prior to that, I did not care much about life, people, myself, or the environment. I simply "existed" because I bought into the false theology that man was nothing; we have no significance; we are unworthy, like the ash that lingers after a fire.

My heart would not allow that to be my reality, so it kept asking questions I could not answer, and no one around me seemed to have the answer, so eventually, when I could not ignore the subtle promptings of my own heart, I went in search of truth. I had no idea what my quest would reveal, but I am grateful every day for embarking on such a journey. The paragraphs that follow are a summation of my personal discoveries without revealing too much.

There is a divine purpose and destiny embedded in each of our lives. We were born into this world to win, to conquer, and to overcome. The very means by which we were conceived speaks to our resilience. The reality is, until we begin to walk in what we believe God has called us to do, there is very little fulfillment for us to experience. I had an idea of what I was called to do, but there was a cloud of uncertainty, fear, doubt, and just not wanting to take the risk to step out. The dream that God gives you will always be bigger than you. That is intentional because it means you will not, and cannot, do it without Him. The next thing is, you will not necessarily be privileged with the information to know where you are going, how you are going to get there, and even if the resources you have can get you there. Even worse, you will feel unqualified to do what God has called you to do.

Here is my experience: make that leap of faith and you will see that the resources come; divine favor is released; you begin to learn from valuable lessons "on the job" and especially from your mistakes; and you will experience exponential spiritual growth in the process. If you never plant the seed in the ground and begin to water and nurture it, it will forever remain just a dead seed. Within that seed is the potential for so much life and fruitfulness, but you must take it through the process for it to fully become what it was intended to be.

Life is uncertain; risk is scary; resources seem limited; God is able, and He says to tell you, "You can do it."

Prayer and Communion

Lord, what is my purpose for being here? I know You know. You created me with a thought in mind. You know what I am truly capable of. You said I can do all things through You. Help me to understand that nothing is impossible for me, if only I will believe. Lord, I believe. Help my unbelief. Direct my steps to walk in the path You have laid out for me so I can fulfil the call that is on my life. Amen.

(Continue praying as the Spirit leads. You can pray in tongues, if you know how. Then take some time to just sit quietly, eyes close, and listen. Silence your mind for a little while and approach the darkness you see without thought, and just listen. You may hear something, or you may not. When you are ready, open your eyes and take communion).

Lord, You said, as I eat and drink the flesh and blood of the Son of Man, I have life in me. Your flesh is real food and your blood is real drink. By eating your flesh and drinking your blood I enter into You and You into me. In the same way that the Father sent You here and You live because of Him, so when I make a meal of

You, I will live because of You. You are the Bread from heaven. When I eat this Bread, I will live always.[45]

Lord, this is Your instruction to me. On the night of Your betrayal, you took bread. Having given thanks, You broke it and said, "This is my body, broken for you. Do this to remember me." After supper, You did the same thing with the cup: "This cup is my blood, my new covenant with you. Each time you drink this cup, remember me."

I declare that every time I eat this bread and drink this cup, I reenact in words and actions Your death, Lord. I will be drawn back to this meal again and again until You return. By faith, I eat Your body and drink Your blood.[46]

---

[45] see John 6:53-58 - MSG
[46] see 1 Corinthians 11:24-28 - MSG

Day 24
Shifting Dimensions

There is a lot to learn from being exposed to different levels of teaching and preaching. Some believe that we must speak at the level of our listeners so what we share does not fly over their heads. I used to believe this as well, until I heard a very famous preacher say that he would never speak at a certain level to his congregation; he chooses to speak to them as if they were college students. He has seen the fruit of this practice over several decades of taking this approach where members of his congregation have ascended to the level at which he teaches.

Congregations today are mixed and dynamic. For the most part, some churches tend to draw only a certain caliber of people. We don't read a lot of books, so we lack the knowledge that the knowledgeable members of our society possess, and we will not win in a verbal debate with them because we will not be able to relate to their level of reasoning and understanding. They have read the Bible too, but are usually more preoccupied with the many contradictions they believe it contains, and they have read many other books too. It is sad that Christians don't value knowledge as much as the world, but it is insane to think that we can win them to Christ with a few rehearsed religious slurs.

If we want people to be transformed, we must set the bar. They do this in schools. When we shift from one grade to a new grade, the level of teaching and expectation is much higher than where we are coming from. Teachers and Lecturers will not stoop to the level we were, because then we would get stuck there. They will be forbearing and understanding when we grapple with the new information, but the expectation is always growth and a higher ascendency of our thought patterns and reasoning and understanding capabilities, and this is the path of growth. We cannot undermine this process when it comes to church, and that is why we have so many infants in our churches.

Another aspect of growth that we overlook is the dealing with self. I have held church positions and functions in the church, and there is this 'culture' where we tend to sweep the issues we have to deal with under the rug for a brief time, so we can perform at church. In other words, we assume a posture of religiosity as we approach the doors of the church, but outside our grand performance in a church service setting, we struggle with our emotions and desires, we backbite, gossip, fall to all manner of sin, and indulge in a myriad of other practices that diminishes our spirituality. This has become the norm for 'church people.'

For us to shift dimensions, there must be constant introspection. The Bible says it like this: "Examine yourself." David said it like this: "Lord, search me. See if there be any wicked ways in me." There must be a revelation of the darkness and evil within, for this must be exposed to the light for there to be total liberty of the living soul of whom we have become in Christ. If we disregard this process, our spirituality becomes truncated, and our power and authority as a son of God is diminished. One solution to this problem is that teachers and preachers must first deal with themselves, and then they must speak at the level to which their listeners need to aspire to reach.

Prayer and Communion

Lord, create in me a clean heart and renew a right spirit within me. Cast me not away from Thy presence or take Your Holy Spirit from me. Restore to me the joy of Thy salvation. Search me, oh Lord, and know my heart today. Try me, oh Saviour, know my thoughts I pray. See if there be, some wicked ways in me. Cleanse me from every sin and set me free. Amen.

(Continue praying as the Spirit leads. You can pray in tongues, if you know how. Then take some time to just sit quietly, eyes close, and listen. Silence your mind for a little while and approach the darkness you see without thought, and just listen. You may hear

something, or you may not. When you are ready, open your eyes and take communion).

Lord, You said, as I eat and drink the flesh and blood of the Son of Man, I have life in me. Your flesh is real food and your blood is real drink. By eating your flesh and drinking your blood I enter into You and You into me. In the same way that the Father sent You here and You live because of Him, so when I make a meal of You, I will live because of You. You are the Bread from heaven. When I eat this Bread, I will live always.[47]

Lord, this is Your instruction to me. On the night of Your betrayal, you took bread. Having given thanks, You broke it and said, "This is my body, broken for you. Do this to remember me." After supper, You did the same thing with the cup: "This cup is my blood, my new covenant with you. Each time you drink this cup, remember me."

I declare that every time I eat this bread and drink this cup, I reenact in words and actions Your death, Lord. I will be drawn back to this meal again and again until You return. By faith, I eat Your body and drink Your blood.[48]

---

[47] see John 6:53-58 - MSG
[48] see 1 Corinthians 11:24-28 - MSG

Day 25
Pursuing Truth

After over a decade of pursuing truth; seeking and searching and praying for direction, I have accumulated more knowledge that I can assimilate in one lifetime. I assume that much of what I know will carry over, unless I tap into immortality on this side of life (which I believe is possible), and outlive my days. That is not a bad thought actually. There have been those who have attained such a reality, and I pay close attention to the lives of those we know about. Yet, with all my studying and pursuit, and after many, many hours of sitting under some really impactful teaching and preaching from some of the leading Christian mystics of our time, and those who have gone ahead (presumably), I still hold a posture that I "know nothing." The challenge is, when I meet someone who knows less than I do because they have never been exposed to the knowledge I now have, and they pretend to know everything: that is a problem.

Our belief system is not as important as we think it is, if pursuing truth is our goal. We just need to ensure that at our foundation is our faith in Jesus Christ, and the work He completed on our behalf. That never changes.

But our approach to faith, language, doctrine, theology, and everything else relating to our journey of faith will grow. There is no contradiction, though it may appear as such, but we know that the language and level of understanding of a baby is quite different from that of an adult. We must never lose our posture to be teachable because unless we are doing exactly what Jesus did, and even greater than that, then we have not yet attained the "perfection" the Bible calls us to. This perfection speaks to maturity as a son of God and has nothing to do with anything we can achieve in our own strength and by our own efforts.

We go to school to learn. We are taught by well-qualified instructors. But how the process by which being taught shifts us mentally and in terms of growth and development, we don't really know. It is a mystery how an influx of information can move us from one level to a higher level of learning, which suggests that the best posture we can assume in this life is to always be teachable. Not in the sense that we only listen to those we deem more qualified based on the level of education that they have attained, but God can use anyone to speak on His behalf, and we cannot always tell when He is speaking to us through someone, so we must learn to listen to everyone.

The pursuit of truth is a never-ending quest into the mysteries and depths of God's very being. It is an adventure, an opportunity to explore through our own active faculties the treasures that are hidden in the darkness we see when we close our eyes. God encounters us every day in one way or form because He loves us, but most of the time, we miss Him. One mystic believes that every human being encounters Jesus in physical form at least one time in their lives. We can easily miss that moment because we dismiss that homeless guy who was trying to get our attention, the waiter we decided not to tip, the stranger who needed help that we ignore, the child who was naked or hungry, the sick we failed to stop and pray for because of our demanding life and schedule. I believe, with all my heart, that if we pay more attention to even the smallest details of our everyday lives, we will have an encounter with Truth.

I want to say a special thank you for joining me on my crazy journey.

Prayer and Communion

Lord, You said You are the Way, the Truth, and the Life. So a pursuit of Life and Truth is a pursuit of You. As Paul says, That I may know You, the power of Your resurrection and the fellowship of Your suffering. You said, if any will come after You, they must deny themselves, take up their cross and follow You. Lord, today I choose to follow in Your footsteps. If You know

I am unable to deal with some of the repercussions of this decision, then I ask only that You prepare me for what's to come. Amen.

(Continue praying as the Spirit leads. You can pray in tongues, if you know how. Then take some time to just sit quietly, eyes close, and listen. Silence your mind for a little while and approach the darkness you see without thought, and just listen. You may hear something, or you may not. When you are ready, open your eyes and take communion).

Lord, You said, as I eat and drink the flesh and blood of the Son of Man, I have life in me. Your flesh is real food and your blood is real drink. By eating your flesh and drinking your blood I enter into You and You into me. In the same way that the Father sent You here and You live because of Him, so when I make a meal of You, I will live because of You. You are the Bread from heaven. When I eat this Bread, I will live always.[49]

Lord, this is Your instruction to me. On the night of Your betrayal, you took bread. Having given thanks, You broke it and said, "This is my body, broken for you. Do this to remember me." After supper, You did the same thing with the cup: "This cup is my blood, my

---

[49] see John 6:53-58 - MSG

new covenant with you. Each time you drink this cup, remember me."

I declare that every time I eat this bread and drink this cup, I reenact in words and actions Your death, Lord. I will be drawn back to this meal again and again until You return. By faith, I eat Your body and drink Your blood.[50]

---

[50] see 1 Corinthians 11:24-28 - MSG

Day 26
Know Thyself

Humanity, such strange beings
Having a mind of their own, not easily swayed
Each man under their own conviction
Unable to be taught anything contrary
Lost in their limitations
Daring to declare they will not surrender
Finitude for infinite knowledge

I start to think we love the little box
we have created for ourselves
And try to fit God into it
I have news for you; He doesn't fit.

We create this fantasy
That something is not, is, but it will never be
We can convince ourselves that
Something that is not working, is, but it is not
You say you are a realist,
But who defines reality really
I find that your version is remarkably different than mine
We both believe we are both right

Oaks of Righteousness

But what if we are both wrong
That's possible, isn't it?

Humanity; such strange beings
Slaves to our own thinking
Cultured by those before us
Who already decided what we would believe
We think we are nothing,
while striving every day to be something
What an unfortunate contradiction

Humanity, denying divinity
denying God
denying self
Establishing a fantasy
Where something is nothing and
Nothing is something

Humanity, wandering around aimlessly
Trying to find significance in dust
Because dust can be seen
We nod when we hear Spirit is real
But we really don't agree
Because from a natural perspective,
Spirit is scientifically impossible.
But how else can you understand the seen
Outside the perspective of the unseen?

Humanity, a waste of potential

We chase fantasies, temporary pleasures
Momentary satisfaction, not fulfilment
What is purpose?
I don't know.
What is your value?
I don't know.
Where did you come from?
Science says we came from nothing,
So we believe we are nothing.
Fearfully and wonderfully made? Yeah right.
This is what they teach and
We silently believe it to be true:
Formed, not created
Evolved, not designed:
We came from monkeys
So we are mindless baboons
Give us a banana and we will do what you ask

Humanity, divinity denied
We are who we think we are
And can never be anything else
The question is: Whose version of You will You
believe and accept?
The world, the systems of the world —
Will you believe them or God?

You see, God adores you
He sees Himself in you
He wants to manifest Himself in you

Oaks of Righteousness

No matter how messed up and lost you think you are
God wants to use you

The enemy wants to abuse you
He wants to take your true potential
And make it his own
But it is you who empowers the devil
You give him your power

You create the world you live in
Because that's who you are
God gave you the power to do it
So if you want it changed, you will have to change it
No one is going to do it for you
You don't believe me, I see
How long have you been waiting for change?
Keep waiting, doubters
Believers, you stand up
Know yourself—find yourself in God
That's where your identity lies

Humanity, God's prized possessions
A devil's worst nightmare
But if you don't know this to be true
It will not be
If you believe you can't, you won't
If you believe you can, you will
If you believe God, there is no such thing as impossible

Dream bigger
Aim higher
God lives in you—know thyself

Prayer and Communion

Lord, help me to know You as I am known by You. You know my true potential. You know what I am capable of. I doubt myself because I was taught not to believe in myself, but today I shake off all the false ideas of who I am to embrace who I am in You. Lord, help me to know my identity in You. I am not who I think I am. I am not who others say I am. I am who You say I am. Give me the boldness to believe it. Amen.

(Continue praying as the Spirit leads. You can pray in tongues, if you know how. Then take some time to just sit quietly, eyes close, and listen. Silence your mind for a little while and approach the darkness you see without thought, and just listen. You may hear something, or you may not. When you are ready, open your eyes and take communion).

Lord, You said, as I eat and drink the flesh and blood of the Son of Man, I have life in me. Your flesh is real food and your blood is real drink. By eating your flesh and drinking your blood I enter into You and You into me. In the same way that the Father sent You here and You live because of Him, so when I make a meal of

145

You, I will live because of You. You are the Bread from heaven. When I eat this Bread, I will live always.[51]

Lord, this is Your instruction to me. On the night of Your betrayal, you took bread. Having given thanks, You broke it and said, "This is my body, broken for you. Do this to remember me." After supper, You did the same thing with the cup: "This cup is my blood, my new covenant with you. Each time you drink this cup, remember me."

I declare that every time I eat this bread and drink this cup, I reenact in words and actions Your death, Lord. I will be drawn back to this meal again and again until You return. By faith, I eat Your body and drink Your blood.[52]

---

[51] see John 6:53-58 - MSG
[52] see 1 Corinthians 11:24-28 - MSG

Day 27
Is God In Control: Possessing Our Land

T he Israelite Nation is a fascinating study in trying to answer the question: "Is God In Control?" We can begin where Moses was approached by God in the Burning Bush. It becomes known that all his years in Pharaoh's house and in the backside of the desert was preparing him for that moment. God had a very special assignment for him, and the Bible records that God even became upset when Moses tried to convince Him to find someone else.

Fast forward, Moses accepts his mission, and He goes down to Egypt to confront Pharaoh, and apparently the ten known gods of the Egyptians. It was God's intention to prove those gods futile in comparison to Him by challenging and defeating their power. It also very quickly becomes evident that God was not going to do that without the participation of humanity. So, for each plague that was unleashed on the Egyptian community, Moses had to do something:

Then the Lord spoke to Moses, "Say to Aaron, 'Take your rod and stretch out your hand over the waters of Egypt, over their streams, over their rivers, over their ponds, and over all their pools of water, that they may become blood. And there shall be blood throughout all the land of Egypt, both in buckets of wood and pitchers of stone.'" (Exodus 7:19).

Then the Lord spoke to Moses, "Say to Aaron, 'Stretch out your hand with your rod over the streams, over the rivers, and over the ponds, and cause frogs to come up on the land of Egypt.'" (Exodus 8:5).

So the Lord said to Moses, "Say to Aaron, 'Stretch out your rod, and strike the dust of the land, so that it may become lice throughout all the land of Egypt.'" (Exodus 8:16).

And the Lord said to Moses, "Rise early in the morning and stand before Pharaoh as he comes out to the water. Then say to him, 'Thus says the Lord: "Let My people go, that they may serve Me."' (Exodus 8:20).

Then the Lord said to Moses, "Go in to Pharaoh and tell him, 'Thus says the Lord God of the Hebrews:

"Let My people go, that they may serve Me." (Exodus 9:1).

So the Lord said to Moses and Aaron, "Take for yourselves handfuls of ashes from a furnace, and let Moses scatter it toward the heavens in the sight of Pharaoh." (Exodus 9:8).

Then the Lord said to Moses, "Stretch out your hand toward heaven, that there may be hail in all the land of Egypt—on man, on beast, and on every herb of the field, throughout the land of Egypt." (Exodus 9:22).

Then the Lord said to Moses, "Stretch out your hand over the land of Egypt for the locusts, that they may come upon the land of Egypt, and eat every herb of the land—all that the hail has left." (Exodus 10:12).

Then the Lord said to Moses, "Stretch out your hand toward heaven, that there may be darkness over the land of Egypt, darkness which may even be felt." (Exodus 10:21).

Then Moses called for all the elders of Israel and said to them, "Pick out and take lambs for yourselves according to your families, and kill the Passover lamb. And you shall take a bunch of

hyssop, dip it in the blood that is in the basin, and strike the lintel and the two doorposts with the blood that is in the basin. And none of you shall go out of the door of his house until morning. For the Lord will pass through to strike the Egyptians; and when He sees the blood on the lintel and on the two doorposts, the Lord will pass over the door and not allow the destroyer to come into your houses to strike you. And you shall observe this thing as an ordinance for you and your sons forever. It will come to pass when you come to the land which the Lord will give you, just as He promised, that you shall keep this service. (Exodus 13:21-25).

God did nothing without the active participation of His sons on the earth. Note the promise in Exodus 13:25, **"...when you come to the land which the Lord will give you."**

So, there was a promise made to the children of Israel that God would give them a land of their own. They embarked on a journey towards that land, but because of the stubbornness of their hearts, that generation never made it into the promised land. But while the generation after them inherited the promise, they had to participate fully in its fulfillment. This is what was said of the land God had given to His children:

And they gave the children of Israel a bad report of the land which they had spied out, saying, "The land through which we have gone as spies is a land that devours its inhabitants, and all the people whom we saw in it are men of great stature. There we saw the giants (the descendants of Anak came from the giants); and we were like grasshoppers in our own sight, and so we were in their sight." (Numbers 13:32-33).

God had already spoken. The land belonged to the children of Israel. But the land was occupied by great warriors and enemies of God. In order for the people of God to possess what was already theirs by prophetic annunciation from God's mouth, they had to fight and rid the land of the people occupying it.

Did God fight for them? Yes. Did the people sit back and relax while God did everything for them? No. Remarkably, throughout Scripture, we notice more of a partnership between God and man; a mutual and equally beneficial agreement. It was men who put their lives on the line for the fulfilment of a promise that God made to them.

God is in control, yet babies are raped and murdered; the innocent suffer while the guilty go free; and the level of injustice that permeates our societies is erroneous. How can God be in control yet do nothing to stop the many injustices in our society? We act on His authority and by His consent. Thereby, man was given control of the earth, and we need to accept responsibility for the chaos that ensues in our world. If the chaos in our world is man's doing, then it must be man's undoing.

Prayer and Communion

Lord, I know that You are in control, but I also have a role to play. Help me to see prayer as not just trying to get You to act on my behalf, but receiving instructions that if obeyed, will yield manifestation. Help me to listen and to hear as much as I speak so I can participate in enforcing Your will and desires here on earth. Amen.

(Continue praying as the Spirit leads. You can pray in tongues, if you know how. Then take some time to just sit quietly, eyes close, and listen. Silence your mind for a little while and approach the darkness you see without thought, and just listen. You may hear something, or you may not. When you are ready, open your eyes and take communion).

Lord, You said, as I eat and drink the flesh and blood of the Son of Man, I have life in me. Your flesh is real food and your blood is real drink. By eating your flesh and drinking your blood I enter into You and You into me. In the same way that the Father sent You here and

152

You live because of Him, so when I make a meal of You, I will live because of You. You are the Bread from heaven. When I eat this Bread, I will live always.[53]

Lord, this is Your instruction to me. On the night of Your betrayal, you took bread. Having given thanks, You broke it and said, "This is my body, broken for you. Do this to remember me." After supper, You did the same thing with the cup: "This cup is my blood, my new covenant with you. Each time you drink this cup, remember me."

I declare that every time I eat this bread and drink this cup, I reenact in words and actions Your death, Lord. I will be drawn back to this meal again and again until You return. By faith, I eat Your body and drink Your blood.[54]

---

[53] see John 6:53-58 - MSG
[54] see 1 Corinthians 11:24-28 - MSG

Day 28
Is God In Control: Before Genesis

This is a question I am sure many people are asking today, "Is God In Control?" Many will argue equally that the answer is both no and yes, but I think presenting the argument to you and allowing you to draw your own conclusions is the best recourse.

So, as we continue this discourse, let us approach this question from both a theological/Scriptural perspective, and from real-life experiences.

Gideon's encounter is a good place to start. This is a fascinating story that I have studied. I like the response of Gideon when he was approached by an angel of the Lord:

And Gideon said to him, "Please, my lord, if the Lord is with us, why then has all this happened to us? And where are all his wonderful deeds that our fathers recounted to us, saying, 'Did not the Lord bring us up from Egypt?' But now the Lord has forsaken us and given us into the hand of Midian." (Judges 6:13- ESV).

Many still ask this question today. According to statistics, over 500 million, at least, of the world's population have chosen Atheism, and I think it is rooted in this question that we seek to answer.

It is never a good practice to make assumptions or to speculate, but I am a highly imaginative person who likes to push the limits of my imagination even beyond its apparent limitations because it is fun, and I can.

In any case, most of the information existing today about humanity's origin, purpose, and evolution is speculation anyway. Some believe in the creation theory, others in the big bang and all other scientific conclusions; still others have found a way to merge all the theories into one, which I find very fascinating, but let's engage our imagination a bit.

If we take all that we know about our existence and put it on a timeline, what is the original starting point? Where did existence and reality begin? Let's take a look at the Bible and argue from that perspective. Genesis 1:1 says: **"In the beginning God..."** There is no explanation given about what could have existed before this moment or where God came from. He just IS! So there is a vast reality behind that moment that just IS, but no one seems to know what that is, what it looks like, how long it has been in existence, or any other question we may be able to attach to that moment.

If God just IS, and He has always been there, with nothing before or behind Him, or no real point before or behind Him, then nothing we know can explain Him. What we know about HIM is based on what is already known, and if He dwells in the realm of the unknowable, then we really don't know Him or can know Him, especially if we measure existence by time, space and matter, because none of this seems to define who God is, or the realm that exists in Him and before Him, even before He said, "Let there be light." That could not have been the first time the Creator spoke. The heavens and earth could not have been the first creation.

We live in a world that we know now based on scientific and geographical mapping and exploration, yet there is no way to know how many worlds existed before this one; how many beings exist outside of human beings; because the answers to all those questions must be infinite as He is infinite.

We are forced then to consider our role only in the context of "In the beginning God" to "A new heaven and a new earth" and not beyond those parameters, because this is the timeline that relates to us because it is where we made our grand, and conscious entrance into existence and reality, whatever that is on a cosmic scale.

Do you see why, no matter how old we are, we cannot lay claim to "absolute knowledge?" We can learn concepts, have experiences, generate personal beliefs and convictions, make something of ourselves that the wider society can benefit from, and we can accumulate a certain measure of wealth, but surely, we must serve a higher purpose than that. *Is God In Control* is a troublesome question to answer, because the next obvious question is usually, "If there is really a God, and He is as good as you say He is, why does evil exist in the world?" It gets challenging to say God is in control when innocent children are raped and murdered, women are physically and verbally abused with no intervention, the guilty get acquitted in our court systems, while the innocent get sentenced, and the atrocities go on and on. How did we get from "and God saw that it was good" to a world in perpetual degradation? Can we ever rise again, when God can look and say, "It is good?" Whose responsibility is it to make it all good again, is the question we must answer. Someone is responsible for what it was, what it is now, and what it is to become, and we cannot escape having this conversation.

Prayer and Communion

Lord, help me to know what role I must play in the rectifying of this broken world. You have called us to be repairers of the breach. In the beginning, You said, take dominion and replenish. We have not done this well since the fall, but You have restored us to our former estate, so now I ask that You teach me how to walk out my call as a child of God. Amen.

(Continue praying as the Spirit leads. You can pray in tongues, if you know how. Then take some time to just sit quietly, eyes close, and listen. Silence your mind for a little while and approach the darkness you see without thought, and just listen. You may hear something, or you may not. When you are ready, open your eyes and take communion).

Lord, You said, as I eat and drink the flesh and blood of the Son of Man, I have life in me. Your flesh is real food and your blood is real drink. By eating your flesh and drinking your blood I enter into You and You into me. In the same way that the Father sent You here and You live because of Him, so when I make a meal of You, I will live because of You. You are the Bread from heaven. When I eat this Bread, I will live always.[55]

Lord, this is Your instruction to me. On the night of Your betrayal, you took bread. Having given thanks, You broke it and said, "This is my body, broken for you. Do this to remember me." After supper, You did the same thing with the cup: "This cup is my blood, my

---

[55] see John 6:53-58 - MSG

new covenant with you. Each time you drink this cup, remember me."

I declare that every time I eat this bread and drink this cup, I reenact in words and actions Your death, Lord. I will be drawn back to this meal again and again until You return. By faith, I eat Your body and drink Your blood.[56]

---

[56] see 1 Corinthians 11:24-28 - MSG

Day 29
Virtue of Love

And over all these virtues put on love, which binds them all together in perfect unity. (Colossians 3:14 – NIV).

I have found myself a little intolerant of being in certain Christian circles because of the hostility, criticism, dislike, intolerance, judgment, and disdain we have for each other. It is just too much. Where is the love? Are we even trying to demonstrate love? Do we realize that human beings are connected, no matter how bad we are, and what we demonstrate to others is actually an attack on ourselves? No wonder our lives don't improve.

Love is the central theme of Scripture and the foundation by which most, if not all, the contributors of the Biblical text were able to move in different spiritual dimensions. Love opens up realms and dimensions for us to gain access because God is love, and God fills all that there is. There is no space in existence that God is not there, and if this is true, then love is the atmosphere, the very air we breathe and, by virtue of love, we can access everything and everywhere. God knows this, so

He commands us to love even our enemies because Love is the principle by which we can access divine realities for us, and the person we direct our love to.

This whole 'judgment movement' is only framing a very dismal future for the next generation. God doesn't need a man to defend Him, so why appoint yourself as His personal defense attorney? God sees all that is happening in the world, and He doesn't always interfere. He knows what is going to transform this world, so He gives us only one command—Love. By virtue of love, you can bring transformation to the things and even the people you don't like.

Prayer and Communion

Lord, thank You for every opportunity You provide for me to demonstrate love. I have acted contrary to Your command on several occasions, and I ask for Your forgiveness. Help me to see beyond people's faults and temperament, to see what You have deposited in them, so I can speak to them and respond to them from that perspective. I seek to be more and more like You, to love more than I speak judgment; to show compassion more than demonstrate hostility in moments of indifference, and to love even those who may not appreciate or deserve it. Amen.

(Continue praying as the Spirit leads. You can pray in tongues, if you know how. Then take some time to just sit quietly, eyes close, and listen. Silence your mind for a little while and approach the darkness you see without thought, and just listen. You may hear something, or you may not. When you are ready, open your eyes and take communion).

Lord, You said, as I eat and drink the flesh and blood of the Son of Man, I have life in me. Your flesh is real food and your blood is real drink. By eating your flesh and drinking your blood I enter into You and You into me. In the same way that the Father sent You here and You live because of Him, so when I make a meal of You, I will live because of You. You are the Bread from heaven. When I eat this Bread, I will live always.[57]

Lord, this is Your instruction to me. On the night of Your betrayal, you took bread. Having given thanks, You broke it and said, "This is my body, broken for you. Do this to remember me." After supper, You did the same thing with the cup: "This cup is my blood, my new covenant with you. Each time you drink this cup, remember me."

I declare that every time I eat this bread and drink this cup, I reenact in words and actions Your death, Lord. I

---

[57] see John 6:53-58 - MSG

will be drawn back to this meal again and again until You return. By faith, I eat Your body and drink Your blood.[58]

---

[58] see 1 Corinthians 11:24-28 - MSG

Day 30
God-Consciousness Versus Devil-Consciousness

The world is changing. If, as sons of God, we are going to be successful in bringing order and realignment from all this chaos, there is a need for us to refocus. The reality is, there are more for us than there are against us. We can't know more about the enemy than we know about those who are for us.

If we are going to change the world, it cannot be business as usual. We need to reject the norm that we know and embrace a new thing. Obviously, all the rituals and traditions we have engaged with for years are not producing the faith and hope needed in the hearts of people for heaven to invade earth. We need God. We need His angelic armies. We need the help of the cloud of witnesses. We need to align with the spirits of just men made perfect. We need to understand principalities and powers (those who did not fall).

Ignorance is no excuse in the age of technological advancement and the increase of knowledge. Whatever state you die in, is the same state you will be resurrected in. The process of spiritual transformation and overcoming that you fail to go through now, you will have to go through it then (after death). Let the just be just still. Let the righteous be righteous still. Let those who are unbelievers, be unbelievers still.

Work on yourself. The Bible says it this way, **"…work out your own salvation with fear and trembling." (Philippians 2:12b).** There is absolutely no way for you to know if what you believe is true, except for the fruit that it produces. Change your focus. Be more aware of the God in and around you, and stop being so engaged with devils.

Prayer and Communion

Lord, I want my focus to be on You. Help me to get rid of everything that would distract my gaze. I know that what I focus on will multiply. The only thing I want to multiply in my life is Your glory and presence, so may my gaze be single to Your glory. Amen.

(Continue praying as the Spirit leads. You can pray in tongues, if you know how. Then take some time to just sit quietly, eyes close, and listen. Silence your mind for a little while and approach the darkness you see without thought, and just listen. You may hear something, or you may not. When you are ready, open your eyes and take communion).

Lord, You said, as I eat and drink the flesh and blood of the Son of Man, I have life in me. Your flesh is real food and your blood is real drink. By eating your flesh and drinking your blood I enter into You and You into me. In the same way that the Father sent You here and You live because of Him, so when I make a meal of You, I will live because of You. You are the Bread from heaven. When I eat this Bread, I will live always.[59]

Lord, this is Your instruction to me. On the night of Your betrayal, you took bread. Having given thanks, You broke it and said, "This is my body, broken for you. Do this to remember me." After supper, You did the same thing with the cup: "This cup is my blood, my new covenant with you. Each time you drink this cup, remember me."

I declare that every time I eat this bread and drink this cup, I reenact in words and actions Your death, Lord. I will be drawn back to this meal again and again until You return. By faith, I eat Your body and drink Your blood.[60]

---

[59] see John 6:53-58 - MSG
[60] see 1 Corinthians 11:24-28 - MSG

Day 31
Face to Face With God

I have a genuine concern about the seemingly "silence" of God in our time and the confusion among those who claim to "hear" and continue to speak. Not that God is ever silent, but I use that term because we are seeking for specific answers, and none seem to be forthcoming.

I believe we have built a culture on using the name of God to forward our own agendas and not spend time to seek the heart of the true God. Nothing shows up our inconsistencies like a crisis, and I have seen the look of despair even on the faces of those I know who know God personally.

My heart weeps at the reality that there are so many people claiming to know God and know what He is saying, when it is obvious that we have lost our capacity to hear God with absolute clarity.

I believe this is the time to seek the heart of the Father. We need to learn like Moses not to do anything unless God goes with us, and however long we need to wait and seek Him before we move, we need to remain in that posture of waiting and seeking so we get back to doing things with God and not just carry out our own misguided and personal will.

I believe this Scripture is yet to be the experience of most believers:

Whenever, though, they turn to face God as Moses did, God removes the veil and there they are—face-to-face! They suddenly recognize that God is a living, personal presence, not a piece of chiseled stone. And when God is personally present, a living Spirit, that old, constricting legislation is recognized as obsolete. We're free of it! All of us! Nothing between us and God, our faces shining with the brightness of his face. And so we are transfigured much like the Messiah, our lives gradually becoming brighter and more beautiful as God enters our lives and we become like him. (2 Corinthians 3:16-18 – MSG).

In our time of crisis, we must now turn away from all that we have been focused on and turn our faces to Him until our own spiritual transformation and physical transfiguration begins.

Prayer and Communion

Lord, I want more of You. Like Moses, I declare, if Your presence does not go with me, then I will not go. Lord, show me Your glory. I have settled and compromised and conformed to the wrong things long enough. Now all I want is You. I pray it's not too late. Amen.

(Continue praying as the Spirit leads. You can pray in tongues, if you know how. Then take some time to just sit quietly, eyes close, and listen. Silence your mind for a little while and approach the darkness you see without thought, and just listen. You may hear something, or you may not. When you are ready, open your eyes and take communion).

Lord, You said, as I eat and drink the flesh and blood of the Son of Man, I have life in me. Your flesh is real food and your blood is real drink. By eating your flesh and drinking your blood I enter into You and You into me. In the same way that the Father sent You here and You live because of Him, so when I make a meal of You, I will live because of You. You are the Bread from heaven. When I eat this Bread, I will live always.[61]

---

[61] see John 6:53-58 - MSG

Lord, this is Your instruction to me. On the night of Your betrayal, you took bread. Having given thanks, You broke it and said, "This is my body, broken for you. Do this to remember me." After supper, You did the same thing with the cup: "This cup is my blood, my new covenant with you. Each time you drink this cup, remember me."

I declare that every time I eat this bread and drink this cup, I reenact in words and actions Your death, Lord. I will be drawn back to this meal again and again until You return. By faith, I eat Your body and drink Your blood.[62]

---

[62] see 1 Corinthians 11:24-28 - MSG

Hidden Treasure

I am making it a practice to hide some gems inside my books as a gift to those who push through to the end. You have done well, and you deserve a reward.

I don't know the circumstances of your conception or birth or the environment you grew up in that shaped your personality and belief system, but I need to tell you that you are not a mistake. You are not an accident. God thought of you before the world was created. You were real in the mind of God. He conversed with You and made wonderful plans with and for you. You agreed to come here knowing you would have a hard life; you just don't have a memory of your interactions with God pre-creation.

God sees and knows you, the real you. Your life may be hard, but you were privy to see the full picture, and you know the end is glorious. That's why Paul could say:

For our light affliction, which is but for a moment, worketh for us a far more exceeding and eternal weight of glory; While we look not at the things which are seen, but at the things which are not seen: for the things which are seen are temporal; but the

things which are not seen are eternal. (2 Corinthians 4:17-18 - KJV).

If you can just get the perspective right, nothing will trouble you. Nothing will shake you. At the foundation of all that we experience in life is God's promise that "It is good."

But we have this treasure in earthen vessels, that the excellency of the power may be of God, and not of us. (2 Corinthians 4:7 - KJV).

Regardless of what you think of yourself, it is God's thoughts about you that matter. He thought you worthy to carry the greatest treasure in all existence: Himself. You are the vessel that carries God. You are the temple where He has made a permanent dwelling. You are worthy of God. He decided that before you were born here and messed up. He decided that before you were conscious enough to fall and make silly choices. Your mess has not changed His mind about you. He loves you because you are just that awesome.

If you so desire, you can connect with the author @
malachicsteele@gmail.com

Please consider leaving an honest review on Amazon
and Goodreads (if you are a member). It really helps
in getting this book out to those who may need it.

www.ingramcontent.com/pod-product-compliance
Lightning Source LLC
Chambersburg PA
CBHW072347090426
42741CB00012B/2959